YOUR RIGHTS

2004–05

A GUIDE TO MONEY BENEFITS
FOR OLDER PEOPLE

SALLY WEST

AGE
Concern

BOOKS

Age Concern England would like to thank the Department for Work and Pensions and the Department of Health for their comments on the text. The author also thanks Sheelagh Donovan, Flavia Gapper, Fran Gonsalves, Ben Moore and Anna Nalecz from Age Concern England's Information Unit for their contributions.

Published by Age Concern England
1268 London Road
London SW16 4ER

© 2004 Age Concern England

Thirty-second Edition

This edition prepared by Sally West

Editor Ro Lyon
Production Vinnette Marshall
Typeset by GreenGate Publishing Services, Tonbridge, Kent
Printed in Great Britain by Bell & Bain Ltd, Glasgow

A catalogue record for this book is available from the British Library.

ISBN 0-86242-393-7

CONTENTS

INTRODUCTION

This book provides information about the main financial benefits and entitlements available for older people. Most of the information applies to those aged 60 and over. The social security rates given generally apply from the week beginning 12 April 2004.

Your Rights is divided into five parts. The first section gives details about pensions and retirement, and the second section is about financial help for those on low incomes. The third section covers benefits for disabled people and their carers, including the system of help towards paying for care, while the fourth gives information about other types of financial help.

Many of the subjects covered in *Your Rights* can be complicated, and the book aims to explain them as simply as possible. However, it cannot cover all situations and circumstances. If you need more information, the fifth section gives details about obtaining relevant leaflets from the Department for Work and Pensions (formerly called the Department of Social Security), Age Concern factsheets and contacting other local and national sources of help. There is also an index and a summary of main benefit rates on pages 198–199.

In April 2002, The Pension Service, Jobcentre Plus and the Disability and Carers Service replaced the Benefits Agency and Employment Service. There is more information about this and how to contact the relevant office on page 167. Older people will mainly deal with The Pension Service – either through a regional Pension Centre or the local service – but when we refer to the 'social security office' in this book we mean whichever part of the DWP is appropriate, depending on your age and the benefit involved.

Please note that although some older people have young families, benefits for children are not covered in this book. People with dependent children or who are under the age of 60 should contact a local advice agency or Jobcentre Plus office for information about benefit entitlements.

Where you live in the United Kingdom

All the information covered in *Your Rights* applies to people living in England. It also applies to Scotland and Wales except where differences are pointed out in the text.

Although there is a separate social security system in Northern Ireland, the social security benefits available are generally the same. However, there may be some differences in the sources of financial help discussed in the section 'Other Benefits and Financial Support' and local and national sources of further information will also be different.

For further information or advice relating to older people living in Scotland, Wales and Northern Ireland, contact Age Concern Scotland, Cymru or Northern Ireland – the addresses are on page 183. Age Concern Scotland and Age Concern Northern Ireland produce their own editions of *Your Rights*.

If you are living in the UK but subject to immigration control, your benefit position may be affected. This book does not provide information about immigration status, so contact a local advice agency if you need further details.

Living abroad

Many of the social security benefits covered in this book will not apply to you if you are living abroad permanently, or they may stop during a temporary stay abroad. In some cases there are special rules for people who live in the European Economic Area (EEA). The EEA is made up of all the European Union countries plus Iceland, Liechtenstein and Norway. The same rules also apply to Switzerland, even though it is not a member of the EEA. Gibraltar is treated as a separate state for social security purposes.

For more information on pensions and benefits for people living abroad, either permanently or temporarily, contact your social security office (if you are currently in this country) or International Pension Centre, The Pension Service, Tyneview Park, Whitley Road, Benton, Newcastle upon Tyne NE98 1BA; this is the part of the DWP that deals with pensions and benefits paid abroad. It produces GL29 *Going Abroad and Social Security Benefits* and a series of leaflets covering social security arrangements with countries outside the UK including Jersey, Guernsey and the countries of the European Union.

Keeping up to date

This book is based on information available at the end of March 2004 and includes the changes announced in the Budget on 17 March 2004. If you would like to be kept up to date with any changes during the year, you can fill in the form on page 182.

A number of proposed changes are mentioned in *Your Rights*. If you need information about the latest position or you have questions on any specific points in the book, please write to Age Concern England at the address on page 183.

Each year the rates of most State pensions and benefits increase, and there are often other changes that affect the financial support available to older people. For example, during 2004 Parliament is due to consider legislation that would enable same sex couples to enter into a 'civil partnership', and this is expected to give registered civil partners many of the same rights to State pensions and benefits as married couples. Information about this and other changes to pensions and benefits will be in the next edition of *Your Rights*, which will be available in April 2005.

PENSIONS

This part of *Your Rights* contains information about the State Pension. There is also a section which describes what is available to people before and after State Pension age.

In addition there are details about the Christmas Bonus (paid to people receiving a State Pension or certain other benefits); the procedure for appealing against a social security decision; and occupational and personal pensions.

STATE PENSIONS

The State Pension is paid to people who have reached State Pension age (currently 60 for women, 65 for men) and who fulfil the National Insurance (NI) contribution conditions. The amount you receive is not affected by your income and savings but it is taxable. You can draw your State Pension even if you are still working.

Your State Pension may consist of a Basic Pension plus an Additional Pension (based on contributions after April 1978) and a Graduated Pension (based on contributions between April 1961 and April 1975). You will receive an extra 25p each week when you reach the age of 80. You may also receive extra pension if you defer drawing your pension. These different parts of the pension are explained below.

Whether you are entitled to a State Pension or not, you may be able to claim other benefits such as Pension Credit, Housing Benefit and Council Tax Benefit, which depend on your income and savings.

See social security guide NP46 *A Guide to State Pensions*.

Equalisation of State Pension age

Parliament has passed legislation to equalise State Pension age at 65 for both men and women. This is to be phased in over ten years starting in 2010. No one born before 6 April 1950 will be affected by these changes.

BASIC STATE PENSION

The Basic State Pension is paid at the same rate to everyone who has fulfilled the NI contribution conditions. The full weekly rates are shown as follows:

2

Single person	£79.60
Wife on husband's contributions	£47.65
Married couple on husband's contributions	£127.25
Married couple (if both paid full contributions)	£159.20

You may hear the terms 'Category A' and 'Category B' pensions. Category A pensions are generally based on an individual's contributions, while Category B pensions are paid to married women, widows and widowers based on their spouse's record. Both types of pension consist of a Basic and/or Additional State Pension.

Who qualifies?

You will receive the full Basic State Pension if you have paid, or been credited with, NI contributions at the full rate for most of the years of your working life. If you have not paid enough, you may get a reduced pension or you may not get a pension at all (see 'Your contributions', pages 8–10).

Normally you need to have satisfied the contribution conditions in your own right; but married women, divorcees or widowed people may be able to claim a pension on their spouse's or ex-spouse's contributions, as explained in the following pages.

Pensions for married women

If you are a married woman and you have paid full contributions for all of your working life, you should be entitled to the Basic State Pension of £79.60 a week when you become 60. If you have paid full contributions for only part of your working life, you may be entitled to a reduced pension. However, any years when you were paying the married woman's reduced-rate contributions will not count towards a pension.

If you are 60 or over but have not paid enough contributions for a pension in your own right, you cannot get any Basic Pension until your husband draws his. When your husband draws his pension, you should claim the married woman's pension, which will be £47.65 a week if your husband has a full contribution record.

If at the age of 60 you are entitled to a pension on your own contributions of less than £47.65 a week, it will be made up to a maximum of £47.65 a week when your husband draws his pension. You will need to make a claim. However, if your own pension is more than £47.65 a week, you cannot get any extra pension based on your husband's contributions.

On top of any Basic Pension you receive, you may also be entitled to Graduated and/or Additional State Pension based on any contributions you have made, as explained on pages 18 and 24.

Sometimes married women who have paid NI contributions in the past but who are not working when they reach 60, do not realise that they may be entitled to some pension based on their earlier contributions. The pension is not awarded automatically – you have to make a claim. So if you think you may be entitled to a pension, and you have not been sent a claim pack, contact The Pension Service. However, you should be aware that if you are already receiving a pension or another benefit, such as a pension based on your husband's contributions or a Widow's Pension for example, you may not be entitled to anything more.

Increases for dependants

Dependent wives

If you are under 60 when your husband draws his State Pension (at 65 or more), and you live together, he may be able to claim for you as a dependant, and his pension will be increased by a maximum of £47.65 a week. However, your husband will not receive any increase for you if you receive certain State benefits of £47.65 or more. The increase may also be affected by any earnings you have. He will not be able to receive the increase if you are working and earn more than £55.65 a week (after certain expenses connected with work have been deducted). Any occupational or personal pension you receive will be counted as earnings.

If you do not live with your husband, he may be able to receive an increase if he is making a contribution to your maintenance. He will not be able to receive this increase if you receive certain State benefits of £47.65 or more, or if you earn more than £47.65 a week.

Dependent husbands

If you are a married man and your wife is receiving a State Pension, she may be able to get an increase for you of up to £47.65, provided you are not earning more than £55.65 a week (£47.65 if you do not live with your wife). However, she can get this increase only if she is receiving Incapacity Benefit with an addition for you immediately before she starts to draw the State Pension. Your wife will not receive any increase if you have a State Pension or certain other benefits of £47.65 or more.

Pensions for divorced and separated people

Divorced people

If you are divorced but do not qualify for a full State Pension based on your own contributions, you may be able to use your former spouse's contribution record to increase the amount of Basic Pension you receive to the maximum pension for a single person of £79.60 a week. You are not entitled to your former spouse's Graduated or Additional State Pension. (However, since December 2000, when rules on 'pension sharing' came into effect, it has been possible for Additional State Pension to be divided as part of a divorce settlement.)

You can substitute your former spouse's contribution record for your own from the start of your working life up until your divorce or just for the period of your marriage.

If you get divorced before State Pension age, you may need to pay further contributions after your divorce to qualify for a Basic Pension. If you get divorced after State Pension age and are receiving the married woman's pension, you may be able to use the rules outlined above to get a full pension.

If you remarry before State Pension age, you cannot claim a pension on your former husband's or wife's contributions. However, if you remarry after State Pension age you will not lose a pension based on your previous spouse's contributions.

See Inland Revenue leaflet CA10 *National Insurance Contributions for Divorcees*.

Separated women

If you are separated and do not qualify for a Basic State Pension on your own contributions when you reach 60, or you are only entitled to a pension of less than £47.65, you may be able to claim the married woman's pension of up to £47.65 a week when your husband claims his.

State Pensions for widows and widowers

This section looks at the amount of State Pension that a widow or widower can receive at State Pension age. For information about benefits for widows and widowers who are under State Pension age, see pages 136–139.

Widows

If you were under 60 when your husband died and you have not remarried, you may be entitled to the State Pension based on his contributions and/or your own, once you reach pension age. The amount you receive will depend upon your own, and your late husband's, contribution record and the age at which you were widowed. If you were 60 or over when your husband died, and not receiving the full Basic Pension, you may be able to use his contribution record to bring your Basic Pension up to a maximum of £79.60.

You may also receive Additional State Pension and/or Graduated Pension based on your husband's contributions, as explained on pages 22–23 and 24.

Once you are drawing the State Pension at age 60 or over, you can remarry or live with a man as his wife without losing a pension based on your previous husband's contributions.

Widowers

If you were widowed on or after 6 April 1979 and do not have enough contributions of your own, you may be entitled to a State Pension based on your wife's contributions provided you were both over State Pension age when she died. You may also inherit some of your wife's Additional State Pension and/or Graduated Pension, as explained on pages 22–23 and 24.

If you do not fulfil the above conditions, perhaps because you were widowed before age 65, once you reach State Pension age in some circumstances you may be able to use your wife's contribution record in order to increase your Basic Pension up to a maximum of £79.60 a week.

Once you are receiving the pension at age 65 or over you will not lose any pension based on your former wife's contributions if you remarry.

Your contributions

This section explains the contribution conditions for the Basic Pension. Your contribution record will depend on the NI contributions you have paid and any 'credits' you received for periods when you could not work.

Until April 2000 people paid NI contributions if their earnings were equal to or above a certain level known as the 'Lower Earnings Limit'. Since April 2000 the starting point for paying contributions has been higher than the Lower Earnings Limit. This year, 2004–2005, the Lower Earnings Limit is £79 a week but the threshold for paying NI contributions is £91. However, if you have earnings between £79 and £91 you will be treated as though you are paying NI contributions and will still be building up entitlement to the Basic Pension and other contributory benefits. When reference is made in this book to people who have 'paid' NI contributions, this includes people with earnings between £79 and £91 a week.

There are two conditions that you must meet in order to receive a pension. The first condition is that you have paid sufficient contributions during at least one year in your working life since 6 April 1975 or paid at least 50 flat-rate contributions at any time before 6 April 1975. Credited contributions cannot count towards this first condition.

The second condition is that to receive a full Basic Pension you must have paid or been credited with contributions for 90 per cent of the years of your working life. To receive any Basic Pension at all you must have a minimum number of years' contributions (normally 10 for a woman or 11 for a man).

Whether you will get a full pension depends on your 'working life' and 'qualifying years', and whether your contribution record has been protected by 'credits' and/or 'Home Responsibilities Protection'. These terms are explained below.

If you are more than four months away from pension age, you can check whether you have paid enough contributions to get a full pension by completing form BR 19, obtainable from The Pension Service or by ringing 0845 3000 168.

Both men and women aged 80 or over who have not paid enough contributions for a Basic Pension might qualify for the non-contributory pension described on page 27.

How are contributions paid?

Since April 1975 employed people have paid contributions as a percentage of earnings, and these are collected with Income Tax. Self-employed people pay flat-rate contributions each week which count towards the Basic Pension. If your taxable income is over a certain amount, extra contributions will be collected with your Income Tax.

Which contributions count?

If you paid the married woman's or widow's reduced-rate contributions, these do not count towards a pension in your own right. Contributions made abroad may help you qualify for the Basic Pension if you worked in a European Union country or one which has a reciprocal agreement with the UK.

Working life

Your 'working life' is the period on which your contribution record is based. This normally starts in the tax year (ie 6 April to 5 April) when you were 16 and ends with the last full tax year before your 60th (women) or 65th (men) birthday. A woman reaching State Pension age now has a working life of 44 years and a man reaching State Pension age now has a working life of 49 years.

However, if you were over 16 when the National Insurance scheme started in 1948, you may have a shorter working life – see social security guide NP46.

Qualifying years

A 'qualifying year' is a tax year in which you have paid (or been credited with) enough contributions to go towards a pension.

Since 1978 a 'qualifying year' has been one in which contributions are paid on earnings which are the same as, or more than, 52 times the weekly Lower Earnings Limit. (Between April 1975 and April 1978 the qualifying earnings were 50 times the Lower Earnings Limit.) This tax year, 2004–2005, the Lower Earnings Limit is £79 a week.

Before 1975 working people paid contributions by weekly stamp. To work out your qualifying years before 1975, all your stamps (paid and credited) are added up and divided by 50, rounding up any that are left over – but you cannot have more qualifying years worked out in this way than the number of years in your working life up to April 1975.

See Inland Revenue leaflets CA01 *National Insurance Contributions for Employees* and CA02 *Contributions for Self-employed People with Small Earnings*.

Credits

If you are under State Pension age (currently 60 for women, 65 for men), you may receive a credit in place of a National Insurance contribution for each week you register for Jobseeker's Allowance and are seeking work or you are unable to work because you are sick or disabled or you are receiving Carer's Allowance (which used to be called Invalid Care Allowance). Men aged 60–64 who are not paying contributions will normally receive credits automatically even if they are not ill or signing on as unemployed. However, men cannot get these automatic credits for any tax year during which they are abroad for more than six months.

Late and voluntary contributions

If there are periods when you will not be paying contributions, perhaps because you will be abroad, you may want to consider paying voluntary contributions to protect your pension record. If there are gaps in your contribution record, it is sometimes possible to pay late contributions. However, these must normally be paid by the end of the sixth tax year after the one in which they are due. After the tax year has ended people are usually contacted if they have gaps in their contribution record and invited to pay voluntary contributions. However, these letters were not sent out for the years 1996–1997 to 2000–2001 and so special rules that extend the time limits for paying backdated contributions apply for these years. People who may have missed out are now being contacted. Ask at your social security or Inland Revenue office for more information. If you are not sure whether or not to pay backdated contributions, you may want to contact a local advice agency.

See Inland Revenue leaflets CA08 *Voluntary Contributions* and CA07 *Unpaid and Late Paid Contributions*.

Calculating your pension

To be entitled to a full Basic State Pension, about nine out of every ten years of your working life have to be qualifying years. This means that women with a working life of 44 years will need 39 qualifying years for a full pension. Men with a working life of 49 years will need 44 qualifying years for a full pension.

If you are not entitled to the full Basic Pension, you may get a reduced one provided you have at least a quarter of the qualifying years you need for a full pension.

Example

Christina Paretsky was born on 10 August 1944 and was 16 in 1960. Her working life runs from 6 April 1960 to 5 April 2004, a total of 44 years. To receive a full Basic Pension, she needs 39 or more qualifying years. If she has worked and paid contributions for only 20 years of her working life, she will receive about half the Basic Pension.

Home Responsibilities Protection

Home Responsibilities Protection (HRP) started in 1978 to protect the contribution record of people caring for a child or a sick or disabled person. It helps protect your Basic State Pension and since 6 April 2002 may help you build up additional State Pension through the State Second Pension (see page 19).

You cannot get HRP for the years when you were looking after someone before April 1978. A married woman or widow cannot get HRP for any tax year in which she, if she was working, would only be due to pay reduced-rate NI contributions.

You are entitled to HRP if you meet any of the following conditions, or in some situations a combination of them, for a whole tax year (but note that the rules changed in 1988 for the third condition):

- You get Child Benefit for a child under 16.
- You get Income Support because you are looking after someone and therefore do not need to register for Jobseeker's Allowance.

- For at least 35 hours a week you look after someone who receives, for a minimum of 48 weeks in the year, Attendance Allowance, the middle or highest rate of the care component of Disability Living Allowance, or Constant Attendance Allowance. For tax years before 6 April 1988, the allowance had to be paid for 52 weeks.
- You are a foster parent (for years from 2003–2004 onwards).

If you get Carer's Allowance (which used to be called Invalid Care Allowance), you will normally be getting NI credits towards your pension so you will not need HRP, although you cannot get credits if you retained the right to pay the married woman's reduced-rate contributions.

How to work it out

HRP makes it easier for you to qualify for a Basic State Pension. Each year of 'home responsibility' will be taken away from the number of qualifying years you need to get a full Basic Pension. However, HRP cannot be used to reduce the number of qualifying years to below 20.

Example

Eileen Smith, who was born in 1944, started work at 16 and paid full contributions for 30 years until 1990 when she gave up work to look after her mother. She was still caring for her mother when she became 60 in 2004 so her pension was worked out in the following way:

Working life	44 years
Number of qualifying years needed for a full Basic Pension	39 years
Number of years of HRP	14 years
Number of qualifying years needed for a full Basic Pension after taking away years of HRP	25 years

Normally Eileen would need to have paid contributions for 39 years in order to receive a full Basic Pension. However, because her 14 years of HRP reduce the number of qualifying years she needs to 25, she is entitled to the full Basic Pension although she has paid only 30 years of contributions.

When to claim

HRP should be given automatically if you qualify under the first two conditions described above. You should not have to claim.

You must claim HRP if you qualify under the third or fourth condition – because you are looking after someone who is getting one of the allowances mentioned above, such as Attendance Allowance, or because you are a foster parent – or if you qualify under one condition for part of the tax year and under another for the rest of the year. Claims for HRP in respect of caring years prior to 2002–2003 can be made at any time up to State Pension age. However, for years from April 2002 onwards you will need to claim by the end of the third year following the year for which you are claiming HRP. For example, for caring during the 2003–2004 tax year you should claim between 6 April 2004 and 5 April 2007. Ask for leaflet CF411 from your social security or Jobcentre Plus office.

How to claim your pension

About four months before you reach State Pension age you should be sent a claim pack. You can ring 0845 300 1084 to make a claim over the phone or to ask for a claim form. If you have not been contacted about claiming your State Pension three months before your birthday, contact The Pension Service or ring 0845 300 1084. A married woman claiming a State Pension on her husband's contributions will need to make a separate claim.

You may decide not to draw your State Pension at 60 (women) or 65 (men) in order to gain extra pension, in which case, when you wish to start claiming the State Pension, you should contact The Pension Service well in advance. Deferring your pension is explained on pages 25–27.

Once you reach the age of 65 (women) or 70 (men), you should claim your State Pension as you will gain no further increases. If you make a late claim for your State Pension, it can only be backdated for up to three months. If Parliament approves the changes referred to on page 25, from April 2005 people will be able to backdate their pension for longer and will have different options if they do not draw their pension at State Pension age.

How your pension is paid

At the time of writing (March 2004) people can choose whether to receive their State Pension and benefits using an order book which is cashed weekly at the post office or to have payments directly into a bank or building society account. The Government wants to change the system, however, so that by 2005 nearly everyone will have payment directly into an account (this is called 'Direct Payment').

The change is being phased in and by 2005 you will receive a letter giving information about the different types of bank, building society and post office accounts. It will be possible for you to choose one that still enables you to get your money at the post office each week. However, some of the arrangements have not been worked out yet – for example, it appears that none of the accounts available at the time of writing will allow you to nominate someone to collect your money from the post office on your behalf on a casual or one-off basis. If you receive a letter inviting you to change the way your pension and benefits are paid and you are not sure which, if any, of the options are suitable, contact a local advice agency. You will continue to receive your money by order book unless you choose to have your money paid into an account at least until Autumn 2004. The Government recognises that not everyone will be able to use an account and there will be a different service for people for whom Direct Payment is not appropriate. At the time of writing further details are not available, but you can contact Age Concern at the address on page 183 or The Pension Service for the latest information about this service.

Until April 2003, if you had your pension paid into a bank, building society account or post office account, it was normally paid four-weekly or quarterly in arrears but under the new system you can receive it paid weekly into an account. If your payment is currently four-weekly and you would prefer weekly payments, contact The Pension Service to ask if you can change.

Pay-day for anyone who started to draw their pension before 28 September 1984 is normally Thursday. For people who retired after that date, pay-day is usually Monday, although if your spouse is already receiving a pension on Thursday, you can choose to have yours on the same day. You cannot receive any pension for days of retirement before your first pay-day.

Most pensions of £5 a week or less are paid once a year, in December, in arrears. If you receive payment by Direct Payment, you will be paid by that method; if you receive payment by order book, you will be paid by crossed payable order.

See social security leaflet DPL1 *Direct Payment: Giving It to You Straight* or ring the Direct Payment Info Line on 0800 107 2000.

Going abroad or living there

If you receive your State Pension by weekly order book and are going abroad for less than three months, you can cash your pension orders when you come home. However, a pension order cannot be cashed more than three months after the date printed on it. If you are going abroad for longer, tell The Pension Service well in advance so that your pension can be paid into a bank or other account while you are away. Alternatively, you may arrange for your pension to accrue and be paid in one lump sum on your return. If you do not receive your pension by weekly order book, you do not need to tell The Pension Service unless you are staying abroad for more than six months. You can, if you wish, arrange to receive your pension in the country where you are staying. If you remain abroad, the annual pension increase will be paid only if you are living in a European Union country or in a country with which the UK has special arrangements.

Contact your social security office or International Pension Centre, The Pension Service, Tyneview Park, Whitley Road, Benton, Newcastle upon Tyne NE98 1BA.

Going into hospital

If you go into hospital you will normally continue to receive your full State Pension for up to 52 weeks (before April 2003 the pension was reduced after six weeks). However, it may be reduced before 52 weeks if you go into hospital within 28 days of a previous stay as the periods in hospital are added together.

After 52 weeks in hospital your pension is reduced to £15.90 a week if you are single. If you are married and your husband or wife is at home, after 52 weeks in hospital your pension is reduced by £30.25. You will normally be paid £15.90 of the pension and, if you agree, any remaining pension will be paid to your husband or wife.

See social security leaflet GL12 *Going into Hospital?*

17

If you disagree with a decision

If you think that you have been awarded the wrong amount of pension, or disagree with another decision to do with your pension, you can either ask for the decision to be revised or appeal against it. Further details are given on pages 32–36.

ADDITIONAL STATE PENSION

This scheme started on 6 April 1978. From 1978 to April 2002, Additional State Pension was built up under the State Earnings-Related Pension Scheme (SERPS) but in April 2002 the State Second Pension (S2P) replaced SERPS.

When you receive your State Pension you may receive Additional Pension on top of your Basic Pension or you may qualify for an Additional Pension even if you do not receive any Basic Pension. The Additional Pension is taxable.

The Additional State Pension is based on earnings, and on any credited earnings that some carers and disabled people have been entitled to following the introduction of S2P in April 2002. However, you do not build up any Additional State Pension based on your earnings if you are self-employed, paying the reduced-rate married woman's contributions, or earning less than the Lower Earnings Limit of £79 a week. Employees may also be contracted out of the State scheme, as explained below.

The Additional State Pension is related to your weekly earnings between the weekly Lower and Upper Earnings Limits (£79 and £610 respectively in 2004–2005), or credited earnings under S2P, from April 1978 until the 5th of the April before you reach State Pension age (currently 60 for a woman, 65 for a man). These earnings are revalued in line with increases in average earnings.

Brief information is given below about how the Additional State Pension is calculated but for more information see social security guide NP46 *A Guide to State Pensions*.

SERPS

If you reached State Pension age before 6 April 1999, your total revalued earnings were divided by 80 to give the yearly amount of Additional State Pension. This formula provides a pension based on 25 per cent of earnings between the specified levels. However, changes were introduced to phase in, between 1999 and 2009, reductions to the amount of Additional State Pension people receive. The main aim of these changes was to reduce the maximum level of SERPS from 25 per cent of earnings to 20 per cent for people reaching State Pension age from 2009 onwards (with some protection for years up to 1987–1988). However, as explained below, S2P provides a more generous pension to people with low or modest earnings.

See social security guide NP46.

State Second Pension (S2P)

Since 6 April 2002 the Additional State Pension has been built up under S2P. If you have entitlement under SERPS this will be protected, so if you reach State Pension age on or after 6 April 2003 you may receive an Additional State Pension built up partly under SERPS and partly under S2P.

Like SERPS, S2P can provide a pension based on your earnings. However, it is built up in a way that makes it more generous than SERPS for people earning up to £26,600 (in 2004–2005 terms) with the greatest benefit being for those on low earnings. At some point S2P may move to be a flat-rate pension but probably not for at least five years.

For this tax year, 2004–2005, employees with annual earnings of at least £4,108 but less than £11,600 will be treated as though they have earnings of £11,600.

You will also be treated as though you have earnings of £11,600 if, throughout the year, you are entitled to:

- Carer's Allowance (which used to be called Invalid Care Allowance);
- the long-term rate of Incapacity Benefit (or would be if you satisfied the contribution conditions) or Severe Disablement Allowance (credits for those receiving disability benefits are subject to having made a certain number of years of contributions on retirement); or
- Home Responsibilities Protection (HRP – see pages 12–14) because you are looking after a disabled person or a child under the age of six. Usually people will be credited into S2P automatically although some people need to claim HRP and when this is the case since 2002–2003 you must do this by the end of the third year following the year for which you are claiming HRP.

To qualify for a year of S2P you must fulfil one of the criteria for a whole tax year – for example, you cannot combine different types of caring responsibilities, or be providing care for part of the year and fulfil the disability conditions for the rest of the year. You will build up about £1 a week of S2P for each full tax year that you fulfil one of the conditions.

Contracting out of S2P

'Contracting out' means that you leave the Additional State Pension by joining either an occupational pension scheme, a stakeholder pension scheme or a personal pension scheme. These schemes have to satisfy certain conditions in order for them to be able to contract out of the State scheme.

If you contract out through your employer's occupational pension scheme, this will provide a pension in place of the Additional State Pension, and both you and your employer will pay a lower rate of NI contributions. If your employer's occupational scheme is not contracted out, both you and your employer will pay full-rate NI contributions and you will build up entitlement to both the full Additional State Pension and the pension due under the rules of your employer's scheme. An adjustment may be made to your occupational pension in respect of any Additional State Pension that you build up during the period that you are a member of your employer's scheme. Contact your employer or the scheme administrator if you need more information.

If you contract out with a personal pension or a stakeholder pension, once a year the Inland Revenue will pay a rebate of your NI contributions direct to your pension provider, together with tax relief at the basic rate on your share of the rebate. These payments are known as 'Minimum Contributions'.

See Inland Revenue leaflet CA17 *Employees' Guide to Minimum Contributions*. Copies are available from the Inland Revenue National Insurance Contributions Office on 0845 915 0150 or on the website at www.inlandrevenue.gov.uk/leaflets/nic.htm

---

Anyone earning below £11,600 in the 2004–2005 tax year will receive a 'top-up' of the Additional State Pension irrespective of whether or not they are contracted out.

It is a good idea to seek professional financial advice before contracting out, especially if you are considering entering a money-purchase scheme or taking out an appropriate personal pension. It is also important that you continue to review your pension arrangements on a regular basis to ensure that you are making adequate provision for your retirement. Again, you should take advice. Remember, however, that if you choose to see an adviser, you may have to pay for their advice.

For more information about different pensions see the Age Concern Books annual publication *Your Guide to Pensions*, details of which are on page 184.

For the period April 1978 to April 1997, any estimate of the amount of State Pension that you will receive when you retire will show how much Additional State Pension you have built up during that period. If you were contracted out of SERPS for any time, the statement will show a 'contracted-out deduction' which takes into account the period when you were not paying into SERPS. The amount of Additional State Pension (before the deduction) minus the contracted-out deduction shows how much Additional Pension will actually be paid on top of your State Basic Pension.

If you are contracted out, any Additional State Pension that you have earned from 6 April 1997 will not be reduced by a contracted-out deduction.

Widows and widowers

When a widow starts to receive her State Pension at 60, or if she is already receiving her pension at the time she is widowed, she can inherit all or some of her husband's Additional State Pension (adjusted for periods when he was contracted out of SERPS/S2P). As a widow any amount you are entitled to is added to any Additional Pension on your own contributions up to the maximum amount of Additional Pension a single person could receive. Subject to this maximum level, the amount of SERPS you can inherit depends on when your husband dies and when he reaches, or was due to reach, pension age (65). A woman whose husband died on or before 5 October 2002 inherits all his SERPS. She can also inherit all his SERPS if he dies after that date but he was born on or before 5 October 1937 (and therefore reached pension age on or before 5 October 2002).

If your husband's date of birth is between 6 October 1937 and 5 October 1945, you will be able to inherit between 60 per cent and 90 per cent of his SERPS depending on his precise date of birth. If he is due to reach pension age on or after 6 April 2010, you will only be able to inherit 50 per cent of his SERPS.

Similar rules apply to a widower if both he and his wife are over pension age when she dies. In this case the husband can inherit some or all of his wife's SERPS depending on when she reaches pension age (60). He will be able to inherit all his wife's SERPS (subject to the maximum level) if she died on or before 5 October 2002, or if she dies after that date but had already reached pension age by 5 October 2002. If a man was widowed on or after 8 April 2001, in some circumstances he may be able to inherit his wife's SERPS if he is under pension age when she dies.

As explained earlier, for contributions made from April 2002 SERPS has been replaced by the State Second Pension (S2P). The maximum amount of S2P that a widow or widower can inherit is 50 per cent, regardless of when they are widowed.

Social security guide NP46 gives more details about how Additional State Pension is calculated, including information about pension rights for widows and widowers whose spouse was contracted out of SERPS/S2P. Leaflet SERPS L1 provides information about inheritance of SERPS.

GRADUATED PENSION

This taxable pension scheme, which is officially called 'Graduated Retirement Benefit', existed from April 1961 to April 1975 and was based on graduated contributions paid from earnings. If you were over 18 during this period and paying graduated contributions, your Graduated Pension for the year 2004–2005 will be based on these weekly rates:

Women	9.63p for every £9.00 contributions paid
Men	9.63p for every £7.50 contributions paid

This will be paid when you claim your pension, normally with the Basic Pension. However, you can receive Graduated Pension even if you do not qualify for a Basic Pension.

Married women, widows and widowers

If you are a married woman of 60 or over and your husband has put off drawing his State Pension, you should be aware that any Graduated Pension you receive – however little – may mean that you will not benefit from an increased married woman's pension when your husband draws his pension. See pages 26–27 for further information.

A widow can inherit half her late husband's Graduated Pension, as can a widower whose wife died after 5 April 1979, provided they were both over State Pension age (currently 60 for women, 65 for men) when she died.

DEFERRING YOUR STATE PENSION

Once you reach State Pension age you can draw your State Pension if you satisfy the contribution conditions even if you are still working. Alternatively, you can choose to defer (postpone) drawing your pension for up to five years after pension age in order to earn extra pension. The Government is proposing to allow people to defer their pension for longer in the future (and to increase the amount that people gain). It has also proposed that in the future people will be given the option of receiving a lump sum rather than a higher pension. These changes are subject to parliamentary approval. If agreed, they are expected to come into effect in 2005.

You cannot normally defer a pension after the age of 65 (women) or 70 (men). However, you may be able to do so if you are a married woman of 65 or over with a husband under 70 who is deferring his pension, as explained below.

You do not have to be working to defer your pension but you will not be counted as deferring your pension if you are receiving certain other benefits instead. For example, a woman who decides not to draw her pension at the age of 60 but to continue to claim Widow's Pension until the age of 65 will not gain any extra pension. You should also note that if you are entitled to an increase for a dependant (for example because you are a married man with a wife aged under 60), this part of your pension will not be increased by deferring your pension.

Even if you start drawing your pension, it is possible to change your mind and defer it instead. However, this can only be done once. If you are a married man and your wife is drawing a pension based on your contributions, you may need your wife's consent before cancelling your pension as she will have to give hers up too.

Increased Basic State Pension

If you defer your State Pension, it will be increased by about 7.5 per cent a year for each full year that you do not draw it. (If you were deferring your pension before 6 April 1979, you will have earned a smaller increase.) For each week that you defer your pension, it will be increased by 1/7p in the pound, but you must defer it for at least seven weeks to gain any increase.

If you put off drawing your pension for the full five years, it will be increased by about 37.5 per cent. For example, in April 2004, the Basic Pension of £79.60 a week would be increased to about £109 a week for someone who had deferred it for five years.

See social security guide NP46 and Age Concern Factsheet 19 *The State Pension*.

Increased Additional and Graduated Pension

If you defer drawing your pension, your Additional and Graduated Pensions will be increased in the same way as the Basic Pension.

See social security guide NP46 for information about the effect of deferring your pension on an occupational pension.

Increased pension for married women

If you are a married woman entitled to a State Pension on your own contributions and you defer drawing it, the pension will be increased as described previously.

If you are aged 60–64 and entitled to a pension on your husband's contributions, you can defer this to gain an increase. If you are 60 or over and your husband is deferring his pension, you will not be able to draw the married woman's pension. Once he draws his pension, you will both receive increases.

However, your pension on your husband's contributions will not be increased if, while your husband is deferring his pension, you draw another benefit such as Additional State Pension or Graduated Pension. It may be better not to draw, for example, a small Additional State Pension if your husband is deferring his pension.

OVER-80s PENSION

This is a non-contributory taxable State Pension of £47.65 a week for people aged 80 or over who have no Retirement Pension. (It is officially called a 'Category D' pension.) For someone who already gets a State Pension of less than £47.65 a week, an Over-80s Pension will be paid to bring that pension up to this level.

To qualify for this pension you have to be living in the UK on the day you became 80 or the date of your claim if this is later, and to have been here for ten years or more in any 20-year period after your 60th birthday. If you have lived in Gibraltar or another European Union country, this may help you satisfy the conditions.

The Over-80s Pension will be counted as income in full for the purposes of Pension Credit, Housing Benefit and Council Tax Benefit.

See social security claim form (with notes) BR 2488.

ENTITLEMENTS BEFORE AND AFTER STATE PENSION AGE

Although State Pension age is currently 60 for women and 65 for men, there is no official retirement age. Some people will stop work before State Pension age and some will work longer, while others may want to retire gradually; for example by reducing their hours rather than leaving work completely. This section summarises the financial support available for people who are not working before State Pension age or who work after that age, referring to other parts of the book where appropriate.

If you are under State Pension age

You cannot draw your State Pension until you reach the age of 60 (women) or 65 (men). However, you may be entitled to other financial support as summarised here.

If you are working

Working Tax Credit started in April 2003 and can provide additional financial help to people with low incomes who work at least 16 hours a week. (See pages 132–133 for more information.) You may also be entitled to help with your housing costs from Housing and/or Council Tax Benefit.

If you are looking for work

If you are able to work and actively seeking a job, you may be entitled to Jobseeker's Allowance, as explained on pages 133–135. You may also be entitled to help with your housing costs from Housing and/or Council Tax Benefit.

If you are unable to work

If you are unable to work because of sickness, you may be entitled to Incapacity Benefit, depending on your contribution record (see pages 107–113). If you are a carer, you may be entitled to Carer's Allowance (which used to be called Invalid Care Allowance) (see pages 102–106). People under the age of 60 who are not required to 'sign on' for work in order to receive benefit may be entitled to Income Support if they have a low income. People over State Pension age and men aged 60–64 can receive Pension Credit without having to be available for work. You may also be entitled to help with your housing costs from Housing and/or Council Tax Benefit.

Occupational and personal pensions

You may qualify for some occupational pension before State Pension age (currently 60 for women, 65 for men) if you retire early. You should check with your employer for details.

You can usually draw a personal pension or stakeholder pension at any time between the ages of 50 and 75. However, if you were contracted out of SERPS/S2P, you cannot start to receive the part of your personal or stakeholder pension built up from the minimum NI contributions paid into your fund until you reach the age of 60.

Protecting your State Pension

If you are under State Pension age and not paying NI contributions, check that you will have enough contributions to receive a full pension when you reach pension age, by contacting the Inland Revenue National Insurance Contributions Office (see address on page 178).

You will receive credits towards your pension if you are drawing a benefit such as Jobseeker's Allowance or Incapacity Benefit. If you are under 60 and seeking work, it may be worth signing on as unemployed – even if you are not entitled to benefit – because you will receive credits. If you are a man aged 60–64, you will normally receive credits automatically even if you are not ill or signing on as unemployed. However, you cannot get these automatic credits for any tax year during which you are abroad for more than six months. If you are not entitled to credits and have an incomplete NI record, you may want to consider paying voluntary contributions.

Working after State Pension age

State Pensions

Once you reach State Pension age you can choose to claim your pension or to defer it (that is, postpone drawing it) in order to gain increases later, as explained on pages 25–27. If you work and draw your State Pension, it will not be affected by the amount you earn or the number of hours you work. You should note, however, that if you are claiming an addition with your pension for a dependent husband or wife, this addition could be affected by their earnings, as explained on pages 4–5.

Although your pension will not be reduced because you are working, it is counted as part of your taxable income. Your tax code will be adjusted to take into account the amount of any pension (including Additional and Graduated) you receive.

If you carry on working after State Pension age, you will not have to pay NI contributions. You should receive a 'certificate of exception' from the Inland Revenue to give to your employer, who will still have to pay contributions for you.

Unemployment and sickness

If you have deferred your State Pension, you cannot claim Incapacity Benefit or Jobseeker's Allowance if you become unable to work. This is because neither of these benefits can start to be paid to someone who has reached State Pension age.

Occupational and personal pensions

If you have a private pension, you may be able to receive this while you are working, but there are rules that will generally prevent you from drawing an occupational pension and working for the same company. This may change in the future – contact your pension scheme for more information.

| CHRISTMAS BONUS

The Christmas Bonus of £10 will be paid to people who are entitled to one of the State benefits listed below and who are living in the UK or any European Union country during the week beginning 6 December 2004. The bonus is tax-free and has no effect on other benefits.

Who qualifies?

You will get the Christmas Bonus if you are receiving:

- a State Pension;
- Over-80s or Widow's Pension;
- Attendance Allowance;
- Disability Living Allowance (any level or component);
- Carer's Allowance;
- Industrial Death Benefit;
- Incapacity Benefit payable at the long-term rate;
- Severe Disablement Allowance;
- Pension Credit;
- War Widow's Pension;
- Unemployability Supplement or Allowance; or

- Constant Attendance Allowance paid with a War or Industrial Disablement Pension.

It is also payable to someone aged 65 or over who receives a War Disablement Pension, but who does not get a qualifying social security benefit.

Only one bonus can be given to each person. However, someone over pension age may get an additional bonus for a dependent spouse or an unmarried partner who is over pension age or who reaches pension age during the week beginning 6 December 2004 but is not entitled to the bonus in their own right, as long as the relevant conditions are satisfied.

How it is paid

There is usually no need to claim, as the bonus is paid automatically. Depending on the way your pension is normally paid, the bonus will be added to your pension to collect at the post office, paid into a bank or building society account, or sent by giro cheque. If you think you are entitled to the bonus but do not receive it by the end of December, contact The Pension Service or Jobcentre Plus office that pays your pension or benefits.

DECISION MAKING AND APPEALS

This section outlines the system of decision making and the way that you can challenge a decision about a State Pension or benefit. There is a different review system for the discretionary Social Fund, which is explained on page 88.

When you receive a letter giving details of whether you have been awarded a benefit, and if so how much, you will also get information about what to do if you disagree with the decision. It is very important to be aware that there are time limits for challenging decisions and you should take action as soon as possible if you are unhappy with a decision.

If you want to challenge a decision it is often useful to get advice from a local agency such as a Citizens Advice Bureau. For example it may be able to advise on whether you have a good case; contact the social security office on your behalf; prepare your case; and it may perhaps be able to represent you at an appeal tribunal.

Decisions

Most social security decisions are made by the Secretary of State – in practice by a decision maker in the social security office on behalf of the Secretary of State. Decisions on Housing and Council Tax Benefit are made by decision makers in the local authority. In most situations decisions can be revised or superseded or you can take the matter to an appeal tribunal. You should note, however, that the information below does not apply to certain types of decision, such as how benefits are paid. These decisions are not subject to the appeals procedures, although you can still ask for the decision to be reconsidered. For some decisions about contributions you will need to contact the Inland Revenue if you disagree with the decision.

Revising and superseding decisions

If you are refused benefit or disagree with the amount awarded, you have one calendar month to ask for the decision to be revised (ie to be looked at again and changed). If you have not been given a written 'statement of reasons' for the decision, you can ask for one within the one-month period, in which case the time limit will be extended by 14 days. If the statement arrives outside the one-month period, the 14 days starts from when you receive it. The one-month time limit can also be extended to up to 13 months in certain situations if there are 'special circumstances' for asking for a late revision.

If you are asking for the decision to be revised you should send in any additional information that might help. Asking for a revision is intended to be a quick and flexible procedure. You can do this by letter or telephone, explaining why you think the decision is wrong – you should make it clear that you are asking for your benefit to be revised. You will then be sent a letter explaining whether the decision is being revised. If you are still not happy with the decision you can appeal.

Decisions awarding benefit may also be 'superseded' at any time if, for example, your circumstances change or there is new information which affects the decision. You should let the social security office know as soon as possible about any information that might affect your benefit. Otherwise you may lose benefit or receive too much and have to repay money.

Appeals

If you have received a decision you disagree with, or you have asked for a decision to be revised and you are not happy with the outcome of that application, you can appeal. You should appeal within one month of the date on the letter about the revision, although this time can be extended to up to 13 months if your appeal has a reasonable prospect of success or there are 'special circumstances' why it is late. If you appeal, the decision will be looked at again to see if it can be revised. If the decision is revised in your favour the appeal will not go ahead, even if you do not get all you asked for. You can appeal against the new decision if you are still unhappy. You should ask for an appeal using the form attached to leaflet GL24 *If You Think Our*

Decision is Wrong if possible (although other requests in writing may be accepted), saying which decision you are appealing against and giving the reasons why you disagree with the decision.

Although most appeals will be considered by a tribunal, there is the option for the Appeals Service to 'strike out' an appeal, for example if you do not provide information requested within the specified time limits. Contact a local agency for help if this happens. When your appeal is accepted you will be sent information and papers relevant to your case. You must let the Appeals Service know if you wish to attend the tribunal or if you want the decision to be made just on the basis of the written information you have provided. It is always better to attend if possible so as to have an opportunity to explain the position and answer questions.

Tribunals

Appeals are administered by the Appeals Service, which is an agency of the Department for Work and Pensions (DWP). Tribunals will consist of one, two or three people, depending on the benefit involved and the issues raised. Tribunal members are independent of the DWP and one will be a lawyer. There may be an officer from the social security office present.

When you arrive at the tribunal, a clerk will explain the procedures, which are intended to be as informal as possible. You will be given time to put your case and the tribunal will ask questions. The clerk should reimburse your travel expenses before you leave. The tribunal must decide whether the decision was right according to the law, but cannot change a decision just because it seems unfair. You may be told the outcome straightaway; otherwise notification of the decision will be sent to you later.

If you are unhappy with the tribunal's decision, you may be able to make a further appeal to a Social Security Commissioner; you should seek advice from a local advice agency about how to do this.

See social security guide NI260 *A Guide to Revision, Supersession and Appeal* or the *Welfare Benefits and Tax Credits Handbook* (see page 181) for more detailed information.

OCCUPATIONAL AND PERSONAL PENSIONS

This section gives brief information about occupational, personal and stakeholder pensions, and where you can get advice if you have a problem. It also summarises how these pensions can affect your State benefits.

Occupational pensions are run by employers and are also known as 'company' pensions. Personal pensions and stakeholder pensions are provided by financial institutions, such as banks, building societies and insurance companies. Employees earning over a certain amount must either pay into the Additional State Pension or be contracted-out into an occupational, personal or stakeholder pension, as explained on pages 21–22. Self-employed people do not have access to either the Additional State Pension or to an occupational pension and cannot, therefore, contract out. They can, however, take out a personal pension or a stakeholder pension that is not contracted out of the State scheme. Stakeholder pensions have been available since April 2001 and are a type of personal pension which must satisfy certain government standards with the aim of providing flexibility and value for money.

It is not within the scope of this book to give information about the different types of pension scheme and, in any case, terms and

conditions vary. You should therefore contact your scheme provider
for more information – for example if you need to find out more about
provision for widows or other dependants.

If you have paid into one or more pensions in the past and have
lost touch with any of the schemes, you may be able to trace them
through the Pension Schemes Registry, PO Box 1NN, Newcastle
upon Tyne NE99 1NN. Tel: 0191 225 6316.

Getting advice

If you have a problem with your pension that you cannot sort out with
your employer or pension provider, you can seek advice from the
Pensions Advisory Service (OPAS – address on page 179) or a
Citizens Advice Bureau. OPAS is an independent voluntary
organisation with a network of local advisers who can offer free help
and advice. If OPAS cannot resolve your problem, it may recommend
that you make a complaint to the Pensions Ombudsman.

See the Age Concern Books annual publication *Your Guide to
Pensions* for further information about different types of pension
(details on page 184). The Department for Work and Pensions
produces a number of leaflets on State Pensions and other
pensions – these can be obtained from the Pensions Info-Line on
0845 731 3233 or the website at www.dwp.gov.uk

How State benefits are affected

An occupational, personal or stakeholder pension will be counted as
income in full for the purposes of benefits such as Pension Credit,
Income Support, income-based Jobseeker's Allowance (JSA),
Housing Benefit and Council Tax Benefit. It can also reduce the

amount of contribution-based JSA you get (see page 133) or the amount of Incapacity Benefit paid (see page 110). If you receive a pension or benefit and wish to claim an increase for a dependent wife or husband, any occupational, personal or stakeholder pension they receive will be counted as earnings and may affect your increase, as explained on pages 4–5.

INCOME-RELATED (MEANS-TESTED) BENEFITS

This part of *Your Rights* describes the benefits that people aged 60 or over may be able to claim based on their income and savings. It covers Pension Credit, Housing Benefit and Council Tax Benefit, which are weekly entitlements, and the Discretionary Social Fund, which provides lump-sum payments for exceptional expenses.

Many older people are not claiming their entitlements. Pension Credit was introduced in October 2003. It replaced Income Support for people aged 60 and over but also extended it, so many more people are entitled to claim – the Government estimates that around half of all pensioners should be getting Pension Credit.

Housing Benefit and Council Tax Benefit were also made more generous in October 2003, especially to people aged 65 and over. However, up to a third of older people who are entitled to benefit towards their Council Tax are not receiving it. Homeowners are particularly likely to be missing out; perhaps because they incorrectly believe that they are not entitled to help. So if you are aged 60 or over, make sure that you are not missing out on the income that is due to you.

PENSION CREDIT

Pension Credit was introduced on 6 October 2003. It is a weekly social security entitlement for people aged 60 and over with low and modest incomes. You do not need to have paid National Insurance (NI) contributions to qualify for Pension Credit, but your income and any savings and capital over a certain level will be taken into account. Pension Credit is not taxable.

It has two parts – the guarantee credit and the savings credit. The guarantee credit has replaced Income Support for people aged 60 and over (Minimum Income Guarantee – MIG). It helps with weekly basic living expenses by topping up your income to a level set by the Government. The savings credit provides additional cash to people aged 65 and over who have income over a certain level, from sources such as pensions and savings. Unlike Income Support, there is no upper capital limit. People may be entitled to the guarantee credit or the savings credit or both.

Around half of pensioners are likely to be entitled to Pension Credit. People aged 60 or over who were receiving Income Support on 5 October 2003 will automatically have been changed over to Pension Credit but other people will need to claim. If you receive Pension Credit and you are liable to pay rent and/or Council Tax, then you are also likely to qualify for Housing Benefit and/or Council Tax Benefit to help with these bills. Even if your income is too high for you to receive Pension Credit, then you may still be entitled to Housing Benefit and Council Tax Benefit. (See pages 63–84 for more information.)

Pension Credit can be paid to homeowners, tenants, and people in other circumstances such as living with family or friends. You can work and receive Pension Credit, although most of your earnings will be taken into account. Once you get Pension Credit, you may also be able to apply for other benefits such as lump-sum payments from the Social Fund (see pages 84–88), while if you are entitled to the guarantee credit you can get help with health costs such as help towards glasses (see pages 155–156) and free dental treatment (see pages 154–155).

People under State Pension age who are seeking work may be entitled to Jobseeker's Allowance (see pages 133–135), while those under 60 who are not able to work, for example due to caring responsibilities or incapacity, may be entitled to Income Support (see pages 135–136). This book does not provide detailed information about the income-related benefits available to people under the age of 60, so if you need further information contact a local advice agency or Jobcentre Plus office.

Who qualifies?

You may receive Pension Credit if you fulfil all the following conditions:

- You are aged 60 or over (65 for the savings credit).
- You income is below a certain level.
- You are habitually resident in the UK and you are not excluded from claiming benefit because of your immigration status. Contact a local advice agency if you need further advice about the benefit position for people who have been living abroad.

For a couple, one of you applies on behalf of both partners – the person who applies must be aged at least 60, although their partner can be younger. For savings credit at least one of a couple must have reached 65. A 'partner' is your husband or wife or someone of the opposite sex who you live with as though you were married. Throughout this section the word 'partner' will be used instead of 'spouse' because you do not have to be married to be treated as a couple. If you live with someone else such as a friend, you can both apply for Pension Credit separately.

How to work it out

To work out if you are entitled to Pension Credit you will need to use the following steps, which are explained below:

1   Add up the value of your savings and, if you have more than £6,000, work out the 'assumed income'.
2   Add up your weekly income, ignoring any types of income which are not taken into account.
3   Check the 'appropriate amount' for someone in your situation – this is the minimum level of income you are expected to live on.
4   Work out the difference between your income and the appropriate amount to see if you are entitled to guarantee credit.
5   If you (or your partner if you have one) are aged 65 or over, check if you are entitled to savings credit by working out your 'qualifying income' and following the calculation set out below.

1 Your savings

Throughout this book the term 'savings' is used to cover savings, capital, investments and property. Savings are assessed in the same way for both the guarantee credit and the savings credit. Some forms of savings, including your home if you own it, are not taken into account, as explained below.

For Pension Credit up to £6,000 savings, and any income you receive from these savings, is ignored (the amount ignored is £10,000 for people in care homes). For a couple, savings are added together, but the limit is the same. There is no upper savings limit for Pension Credit but any savings over £6,000 will be counted as £1 a week 'assumed income' for every £500 (or part of £500) over £6,000. For example, if you have £7,200 this will be counted as a weekly income of £3 a week, while savings of £13,600 will be assessed as an income of £16 a week.

Savings and capital are normally valued at their current market or surrender value. If there are expenses involved in selling them, 10 per cent will be deducted. Most forms of savings and capital will be taken into account, including:

- cash;
- bank and building society accounts (including current accounts that do not pay interest);
- National Savings accounts and certificates (valued according to rules which The Pension Service will explain);
- premium bonds;
- income bonds;
- stocks and shares;
- property (other than your home); and
- a share of any savings you own jointly with other people – these will normally be divided equally by the number of joint owners to calculate your share (get advice if you need to value your share of a jointly-owned property).

Some types of savings will be ignored, including:

- the value of your home if you own it and are living there;
- the surrender value of a life assurance policy (although if a policy is cashed in the money you receive will normally be counted);
- arrears of certain benefits such as Attendance Allowance, Disability Living Allowance or Income Support are normally ignored for 52 weeks from the date you receive them (or if the arrears are £5,000 or over and due to an official error, they may be able to be ignored for as long as you are getting Pension Credit);

- your personal possessions; and
- the £10,000 ex-gratia payment for Far Eastern Prisoners of War (see pages 116–117).

There are also other forms of savings not listed here which are ignored and there are circumstances when property or savings will not be taken into account for a certain period of time – see the DWP leaflet PC10S *A Guide to Pension Credit* for more information.

Deprivation of capital (notional capital)

If you 'deprive' yourself of savings in order to get benefit or to increase the amount of benefit, you will be treated as still having those savings. This is known as 'notional capital'. This might occur if you give money to your family or buy expensive items in order to gain benefit. However, you should not be assessed as having notional capital if you have paid off debts or if your spending was 'reasonable' in your circumstances. You should seek advice if you are refused benefit because of notional capital.

2 Your income

This section explains how your income is assessed for the guarantee credit. For the savings credit you will also need this figure but, as explained later, if you have certain types of income they will be deducted from the total. Below are listed the main types of income that are counted and the main types of income, or parts of income, that are ignored. If you have any income from other sources you will need to check whether or not they are included. Income is assessed after tax and NI contributions have been paid. For a couple, the income of both partners is added together.

Income that is taken into account includes:

- State Pensions;
- occupational and personal pensions;
- income from annuities;
- most social security benefits (but see below for some exceptions);
- earnings (but see below for amounts ignored);
- Working Tax Credit;
- income from boarders or sub-tenants (but see below for parts ignored);
- maintenance payments from a spouse or former spouse; and
- assumed income from savings over £6,000.

Income that will be fully ignored includes:

- Housing Benefit and Council Tax Benefit;
- Attendance Allowance;
- Disability Living Allowance;
- Social Fund payments;
- actual interest or income from savings or capital (interest is not counted as income but once it is paid into an account it will be counted as part of your savings);
- the special War Widow's Pension for 'pre-1973 widows', which is now £62.68 (in addition to the £10 of a War Widow's Pension outlined below);
- voluntary or charitable payments – for example money given to you by a charity, family or friends (under Income Support rules in some circumstances these could reduce your benefit); and
- payments from some forms of equity release schemes which provide an income not based on an annuity.

The following are examples of parts of weekly income that will also be ignored:

- £5 of your earnings if you work and are single;
- £10 of your or your partner's earnings from work (if you both work the maximum is still £10);
- £20 of earnings if you work and you are a carer receiving the carer addition or in certain circumstances when you or your partner is disabled (instead of the £5 or £10 listed above);
- £10 of a War Widow/Widower's Pension or War Disablement Pension; and
- £20 of any payment from a sub-tenant or boarder, and, in the case of a boarder, half of any payment over £20.

Add up your total weekly income, including assumed income for savings over £6,000 but not including any types, or parts, of income that are ignored to give the weekly income used to work out your guarantee credit.

Qualifying income for savings credit

For savings credit only 'qualifying income' is counted. This is the same as the income used to assess guarantee credit but with the following types of income deducted:

- Incapacity Benefit;
- Severe Disablement Allowance;
- contribution-based Jobseeker's Allowance;
- Working Tax Credit; and
- maintenance payments from a spouse or former spouse.

Most older people do not have these sources of income, so all their assessed income is qualifying income. In this case the same figure is used to work out both guarantee and savings credit. However, if you do have one or more of the types of non-qualifying income outlined above (such as Incapacity Benefit), remember that this affects the way that your savings credit is worked out.

3 The 'appropriate amount'

This is the minimum amount of income that someone is considered to need for their day-to-day living expenses. It is officially called the 'appropriate minimum guarantee' but will often be described as the 'appropriate amount' which is the term used in this book. If your income is below the appropriate amount for someone in your circumstances, then you will receive the guarantee credit to bring your income up to this level. For many people a 'standard amount' will apply (officially called the 'standard minimum guarantee') but the appropriate amount can include additional amounts for severe disability, for carers and for certain housing costs. It is possible to receive both the carer and the severe disability addition – for example a disabled couple who provide a substantial amount of care for each other could receive both.

The standard appropriate amounts are:

Single person	£105.45
Couple	£160.95

Additional amount for severe disability/severe disability premium

Within Pension Credit an addition can be added to your standard minimum amount if you fulfil the conditions described below. For Housing and Council Tax Benefit it is called the 'severe disability premium' but the rates and rules are the same. The rates are:

Single person	£44.15
Couple, one person qualifying	£44.15
Couple, both qualifying	£88.30

As a single person you qualify if:

- you receive Attendance Allowance or the middle or highest level of the care component of Disability Living Allowance (DLA);
- you 'live alone' (but see below for the exceptions to this); and
- no one receives Carer's Allowance (which used to be called Invalid Care Allowance) for looking after you.

If you have a partner and you receive Attendance Allowance (or the middle or highest level of the care component of DLA), you will not normally be able to receive this addition because you will not be counted as 'living alone'. However, you can receive it if:

- your partner also gets Attendance Allowance (or the middle or highest level of the care component of DLA) or he or she is registered blind;
- no one receives Carer's Allowance for looking after you; and
- you 'live alone'; ie there is no-one else living with you and your partner other than a person who is not taken into account, as described below.

If your partner also receives Attendance Allowance (or the middle or highest level of the care component of DLA) and neither of you has a carer receiving Carer's Allowance, you will receive the double rate.

Living alone

You will still be counted as living alone in some circumstances when you live with other people. For example, you can still get this addition if there is someone else in your household who also gets Attendance Allowance (or the middle or highest level of the care component of DLA), or with someone who is registered blind, or with a paid helper supplied by a charity, or in some cases where you are a joint tenant or joint owner and share the housing costs. If you are not sure if you qualify, seek further advice as the rules can be complicated.

Additional amount for carers/carer premium

Within Pension Credit a carer addition can be added to your standard amount if you fulfil the conditions described below. For Housing and Council Tax Benefit it is called the 'carer premium' but the rates and rules are the same. The rates are:

Single person	£25.55
Couple, one person qualifying	£25.55
Couple, both qualifying	£51.10

This addition is available to carers who are receiving Carer's Allowance (which used to be called Invalid Care Allowance – see pages 102–106). It will also be given to people who have applied for the allowance and fulfil all the conditions but cannot receive it because they are getting another benefit instead. There is no upper age limit for applying for Carer's Allowance.

For example, if you are receiving a State Pension of £79.60, you cannot be paid Carer's Allowance as well. However, if you apply for Carer's Allowance, you may receive a letter saying that you are entitled to Carer's Allowance but cannot be paid it, which you can show to The Pension Service (for Pension Credit) or the council (for Housing and Council Tax Benefit), so that they can award you the addition/premium.

The carer addition/premium continues to be paid for eight weeks after the person you care for dies, or you cease being a carer for some other reason.

Effect on the disabled person's benefits

If the person you care for receives the severe disability addition/premium (see above), and you are paid Carer's Allowance, they will lose the addition/premium when you receive your first payment of Carer's Allowance. You might be able to receive an extra £25.55 a week through the carer addition/premium while the person you care for could lose an addition/premium worth £44.15. However, they will not lose the addition/premium if you are entitled to Carer's Allowance but cannot be paid it because you are receiving a State Pension or another benefit. If you are not sure whether to claim Carer's Allowance or not, get advice first.

4 Calculating the guarantee credit

Once you have worked out your appropriate amount – ie the standard amount of £105.45 for a single person or £160.95 for a couple, plus any additional amounts because you are a carer, severely disabled or have eligible housing costs (see page 53) – compare this figure with your income.

If your income (including assumed income from savings) is less than your appropriate amount, you will receive guarantee credit to bring your income up to this level. If your qualifying income is more than the 'savings credit threshold' – £79.60 for a single person, £127.25 for a couple – and you are aged 65 or over, you will also receive savings credit.

If your income is more than your appropriate amount you will not get guarantee credit but you may still be entitled to Housing Benefit and/or Council Tax Benefit and, if you are aged 65 or over, to savings credit.

Example

Rose Williams is aged 76, and lives alone in a council flat. Her income is the State Pension of £79.60 a week and an occupational pension of £10. She has savings of £950.

Rose adds up her income

State Pension	£79.60
Occupational pension	£10.00
Total	£89.60

Her appropriate amount is the standard amount for a single person (£105.45).

Rose's income of £89.60 a week is less than her appropriate amount of £105.45. The difference is £15.85. This is how much guarantee credit she will get on top of her State Pension.

Rose is also entitled to some savings credit (see page 55) and to Housing Benefit and Council Tax Benefit to cover all her rent and Council Tax.

Example

Bill and Mary McConnell are a married couple both aged 70. Their joint State Pensions come to £127.25 and Bill gets a pension of £35.70 a week from his old job. They live in their own home and they have savings of £13,000.

Bill and Mary add up their income

State Pension	£127.25
Occupational pension	£35.70
Weekly tariff income from savings	£14.00
Total	£176.95

Their appropriate amount is the standard amount for a couple (£160.95).

Their income of £176.95 is more than their appropriate amount of £160.95, so they do not qualify for guarantee credit. However, they will be entitled to savings credit (see page 55) and Council Tax Benefit to get help with their Council Tax payments.

Example

Andrew Jennings is 80 and lives alone in his own home. His State Pension is £79.85 and he has an occupational pension of £64.75 a week. His savings are less than £6,000. In May 2003 he applied for Income Support but was turned down because his income was too high, although he received some Council Tax Benefit. In October 2003 he had a stroke. He now has difficulty with getting dressed and washed but has been able to continue to live on his own with support. No one receives Carer's Allowance for looking after him. His local Age Concern helped him claim Attendance Allowance and advised him to apply for Pension Credit.

Andrew's income, ignoring the Attendance Allowance

State Pension	£79.85
Occupational pension	£64.75
Total	£144.60

Andrew's applicable amount

Standard amount	£105.45
Severe disability addition	£44.15
Total	£149.60

His income is £5.00 less than his appropriate amount, so he receives £5.00 guarantee credit. He will also receive the maximum amount of savings credit (£15.51) and Council Tax Benefit to cover all his Council Tax.

Help with housing costs

In addition to your standard amount and any additions if you are a carer or severely disabled, your Pension Credit appropriate amount can also include an additional sum for certain housing costs for those who own their property. For tenants, rent and service charges can be covered by Housing Benefit. These additions for homeowners are not included in the applicable amount for Council Tax Benefit. Subject to the restrictions below, if you are aged 60 or over the housing costs which can be included are:

■ mortgage interest;
■ interest on a loan for certain repairs or improvements;
■ ground rent; and
■ certain service charges (but funding for support services now comes through the 'Supporting People' scheme – see page 122).

If the loan is for more than £100,000 or your housing costs are considered too high (taking into account your situation), the amount added to the appropriate amount may be restricted. Payment is only made towards the eligible mortgage interest and does not cover any payments towards arrears, capital or endowment policies. Claimants may have to meet any shortfall in payments, when their lender's interest rate is higher than the Standard Interest Rate, which is used to calculate benefit support. Payment towards eligible housing costs are generally made direct to a claimant's lender.

If you are receiving Pension Credit or have been receiving it within the previous 26 weeks, you may only receive help towards any new housing costs in very limited circumstances. You should seek advice before taking out a loan.

Deductions for people living in your home

The help provided towards your housing costs may be reduced if there is someone else living in your home apart from your partner or a dependent child. This is because people such as adult sons and daughters (often called 'non-dependants') are expected to contribute to housing costs. Deductions are made according to the circumstances of the non-dependant. However, no reduction will be made if you or your partner is blind or you or your partner receives Attendance Allowance or the care component of Disability Living Allowance.

There are no deductions if the person living with you is: a boarder; a full-time student; or is under 25 and receiving Income Support or income-based Jobseeker's Allowance. If the person living with you is aged 18 or over, works 16 hours a week or more, does not receive Pension Credit and has an income of at least £97 a week, the following deductions will be made:

Gross income of non-dependant	Weekly deduction
£97.00 to £143.99	£17.00
£144.00 to £185.99	£23.35
£186.00 to £246.99	£38.20
£247.00 to £307.99	£43.50
£308.00 or more	£47.75

For others aged 18 or over, the deduction will be £7.40. If there is a couple living with you, only one deduction will be made.

Example

Marie Wilson is aged 64 and has a mortgage. Her mortgage interest is assessed as £30 a week, so her appropriate amount is worked out in the following way:

Standard amount	£105.45
Weekly mortgage interest	£30.00
Total	£135.45

Her daughter who is 35 and earns £170 a week comes to live with her. There will therefore be a deduction of £23.35 from the amount allowed for mortgage interest. Marie's total Pension Credit appropriate amount will then be reduced to £112.10. This means that she will receive guarantee credit if her total assessed income is less than this amount. She is under 65 and so is not entitled to savings credit.

5 Calculating your savings credit

If you (or your partner if you have one) are aged 65 or over you may be entitled to savings credit, either in addition to guarantee credit or on its own. The maximum amount of savings credit you can receive is £15.51 for a single person or £20.22 for a couple. This section outlines how the savings credit is worked out and gives some examples. However, the calculation is quite complicated and the examples do not cover all circumstances. If you are not sure whether you qualify, you may want to apply anyway. Alternatively, The Pension Service or a local advice agency may be able to give you an idea of any possible entitlement, or, if you have access to the Internet, you could look at the Pension Credit calculator on The Pension Service website (www.thepensionservice.gov.uk).

As a guide, if you are single and your appropriate amount is the standard amount of £105.45, you are likely to be entitled to savings credit if your weekly qualifying income is more than £79.60 and less than around £144. For a couple with a standard amount of £160.95, you will be likely to qualify if your weekly qualifying income is more than £127.25 and less than around £211.50. The closer your income is to these upper amounts the less savings credit you will receive. If your appropriate amount is more than the standard amounts, you may get savings credit if your income is higher than £144 (single person) or £211.50 (couple).

To calculate your savings credit you need to know the following things:

1 Your 'income'. This is the income used to calculate guarantee credit – ie your total income including assumed income from savings but not including types of income which are ignored such as Attendance Allowance.

2 Your 'qualifying income'. This is your income as explained above minus any Incapacity Benefit, Severe Disablement Allowance, contribution-based Jobseeker's Allowance, Working Tax Credit and maintenance payments from a spouse or former spouse.

3 Your appropriate amount, as explained above.

4 The 'savings credit threshold', which is £79.60 for a single person and £127.25 for a couple (the same levels as the Basic State Pension).

5 The maximum amount of savings credit you can receive, which is £15.51 for a single person or £20.22 for a couple.

Appropriate amount of the standard amount (£105.45 or £160.95)

If your income is less than your appropriate amount and your qualifying income is above £79.60 (single) or £127.25 (couple), you will be entitled to savings credit. Your savings credit will be 60 per cent of the difference between your qualifying income and £79.60 if you are single or £127.25 if you have a partner, up to the maximum amounts. (Another way of saying this is that you will receive 60p for every £1 of qualifying income you have over the threshold.)

Example

On page 50, **Rose Williams** has a Basic State Pension of £79.60 and an occupational pension of £10 a week. Her savings credit will be worked out like this:

Qualifying income	£89.60
Difference between income of £89.60 and savings threshold of £79.60	£10.00
Savings credit is 60% of £10 (the difference)	£6.00

Rose will receive £6 savings credit in addition to her £15.85 guarantee credit and her pensions of £89.60, making her total income £111.45.

If your qualifying income is exactly £105.45 (single person) or £160.95 (couple), you will normally receive the maximum savings credit, which is £15.51 for a single person and £20.22 for a couple. (If you also have some non-qualifying income, you will receive less.)

If all your income is qualifying income and it is more than £105.45 (single person) or £160.95 (couple), you will receive savings credit if your income is less than a certain amount, which is around £144 for a single person and £211.50 for a couple. The maximum savings credit of £15.51 for a single person and £20.22 for a couple will be reduced by 40 per cent of the difference between your qualifying income and £105.45 (single person) or £160.95 (couple). (Another way of saying this is that the maximum savings credit is reduced by 40 pence for every £1 of income you have above these levels.)

Example

In the example on page 51, **Bill and Mary McConnell** cannot get guarantee credit because their income of £176.95 is more than

£160.95 (their appropriate amount). Their savings credit is worked out like this:

Qualifying income	£176.95
Difference between their income and £160.95	£16.00
40% of this difference	£6.40
Their savings credit is the maximum savings credit of £20.22 minus £6.40 (40% of the difference)	£13.82

Appropriate amount above the standard amount

If you receive an addition for severe disability, caring or housing costs (like Andrew Jennings in the example on page 52), you can receive savings credit at higher levels of income. (Examples are not given here but are included in Age Concern Factsheet 48 *Pension Credit*.) It is worked out like this:

- If all your income is qualifying income and it is more than £79.60 (single person) or £127.25 (couple) but less than your appropriate amount, your savings credit will be 60% of the difference between your income and £79.60 (single person) or £127.25 (couple) up to the maximum amount of savings credit of £15.51 (single person) or £20.22 (couple).

- If all your income is qualifying income and it is the same as or more than the standard amount (£105.45 single person, £160.95 couple) but less than your appropriate amount, you will receive the maximum savings credit.

- If all your income is qualifying income and it is more than your appropriate amount, the maximum savings credit of £15.51 (single person) or £20.22 (couple) is reduced by 40% of the difference between your income and your appropriate amount. If the 40% is more than the maximum you will not receive savings credit.

If you have non-qualifying income

If you or your partner receive non-qualifying income, such as Incapacity Benefit or Severe Disablement Allowance, you may still receive savings credit as long as you have qualifying income over the savings credit threshold (£79.60, single person, £127.25 couple). However, the calculation is done a little differently. Contact The Pension Service or an advice agency if you need more information about this or look at the example in the DWP Pension Credit guide PC10S.

Pension Credit for people in different circumstances

Living in someone else's home

If you live in someone else's home as a member of their household – for example, with your son or daughter – Pension Credit will be worked out in the normal way. However, if your son or daughter gets help with housing costs through Income Support, income-based JSA, Pension Credit, Housing Benefit or Council Tax Benefit, this may be reduced because you are living there.

Boarders and hostel dwellers

If you are living in a hotel, guest house or hostel, or in board and lodgings, Pension Credit will be worked out in the normal way. You can claim Housing Benefit towards the rental element of your charges and some services. You will have to pay for meals, fuel and other items that are not covered by Housing Benefit from your weekly Pension Credit.

If you go into hospital

If you go into hospital your Pension Credit guarantee credit will generally continue to be paid at the same rate for up to 52 weeks. (In the past Income Support and State Pensions were reduced after six weeks.) However, if you receive the severe disability addition your benefit will normally be reduced after four weeks and you will also lose the carer addition before 52 weeks.

After 52 weeks in hospital, your appropriate amount will be reduced to £15.90 with no increase for housing costs. If you have a partner, he or she will normally be assessed separately.

Savings credit can continue to be paid if you or your partner go into hospital, but it may stop or the amount paid may change if you were getting an addition for severe disability, caring or housing costs which stops, or if you and your partner start to be assessed separately.

The reductions outlined here may start sooner if your stay in hospital is within 28 days of a previous hospital stay as the periods are added together.

Let The Pension Service know about an admission to hospital that might affect your benefit, and, if your Pension Credit has been reduced or stopped, make sure that you tell them when you go home.

If you go abroad

If you go abroad for a temporary stay then Pension Credit will normally stop after four weeks. If you are planning to go abroad contact The Pension Service to find out more about your position.

Care homes

Pension Credit for people in care homes is generally calculated as described here but see pages 125–127 for the differences.

How to claim Pension Credit

You can claim Pension Credit in a number of ways. There is a special Pension Credit claim line on Freephone 0800 99 1234. Staff can take your details over the telephone and send you the form to read through, sign and return. If English is not your first language you (or someone on your behalf) can ring and arrangements will be made for an interpreter. You can also write for a claim form or obtain it from the Internet (at www.thepensionservice.gov.uk). If you would like to have face to face help with the form, contact a local advice agency or the local Pension Service. You may need to provide information to support your claim, such as details of your savings and private pensions. The Pension Service is writing to all pensioner households about Pension Credit – however, you do not have to wait until you receive a letter to apply.

Backdating

Special backdating rules apply up to October 2004. If you claim before 6 October 2004, your claim can be backdated to 6 October 2003 as long as you have satisfied the conditions since then. If you are not entitled to the guarantee credit, the savings credit will normally be taken into account for Housing Benefit and Council Tax Benefit. However, if you claim before 6 October 2004 and receive a backdated sum these benefits will not be reassessed and you will not have to pay back any money. In some circumstances people entitled to Housing and Council Tax Benefit might actually be better off in the end by delaying a claim for Pension Credit and getting a backdated lump sum. It will depend on your exact circumstances, however, and most people will probably want to make a claim as soon as they can. Get advice if you are not sure what to do.

From 6 October 2004 onwards it had been expected that backdating would be restricted to a maximum of three months. However, in March 2004 the Government announced that entitlement will be backdated for up to 12 months.

Changes of circumstances and reassessments

When you are awarded Pension Credit you may be told that an 'assessed income period' has been set. This will mean that for the time stated (normally a period of up to five years) you will not need to report changes in your 'retirement provision'. By retirement provision The Pension Service means income from sources such as pensions, annuities and savings. Adjustments will be made automatically for regular increases, such as an annual increase in your State or private pension. If you have a private pension you will be asked how it is increased when you apply. You will not need to tell The Pension Service about changes such as an increase in your savings. However, if your income from these sources goes down, you can contact The Pension Service which will reassess your benefit and may increase the amount of Pension Credit. You will still need to report other changes in circumstances, such as getting married, moving house, a change in earnings, or starting to receive certain social security benefits.

An assessed income period will not be set if you are under 65. Even if you are over 65 you may not have an assessed income period in some circumstances; for example if your situation is expected to change in the next year. Sometimes a period of less than five years is set. At the end of an assessed income period your Pension Credit will be reassessed.

If you are not given an assessed income period you will need to report any changes in circumstances that may affect your benefit.

When Pension Credit is awarded you will be given information about what changes in circumstances you need to report.

How it is paid

Pension Credit and the State Pension are normally paid together. At the time of writing you can choose whether to receive your benefits by weekly order book or paid weekly directly into a bank or building society account. However, see pages 15–16 for information about changes, which are being phased in, to the way that pensions and benefits are paid.

If you disagree with a decision

If you disagree with a decision that has been made about your Pension Credit you can ask for the decision to be revised or appeal against the decision (see pages 32–36). You also have the right to ask for more detailed information about why a decision was made.

See Age Concern Factsheet 48 *Pension Credit* and social security leaflet PC1L *Pension Credit: Pick It Up. It's Yours* or the more detailed social security guide PC10S.

HOUSING BENEFIT AND COUNCIL TAX BENEFIT

Housing Benefit provides help with rent, with certain service charges and, in Northern Ireland, with general rates. People who live in Northern Ireland and require information about rate rebates should contact Age Concern Northern Ireland.

Council Tax Benefit is a social security benefit which provides help with paying the Council Tax. See also 'Help with the Council Tax' on pages 149–150, which gives information about other ways your Council Tax bill may be reduced which are not related to your income or savings. The information here only applies to people aged 60 and over. The rules are different for younger people, so if you are under 60 contact your council or a local advice agency for more information.

You should note that when Pension Credit was introduced in October 2003, there were also changes to Housing and Council Tax Benefit rules for people aged 60 and over. As a result some people who previously could not receive these benefits will now be entitled to some help. This is particularly likely to apply if you are aged 65 or over.

Housing Benefit and Council Tax Benefit are based on your income and savings. In general you must have no more than £16,000 in savings, although the limit does not apply to people receiving the guarantee part of the Pension Credit or the second adult rebate within the Council Tax Benefit system. You must also be 'habitually resident' in the UK, and not excluded from claiming because of your immigration status. If you have a partner (that is, you are married or live with someone of the opposite sex as though you were married), the amount of benefit you get will be worked out on your combined savings and income. Housing Benefit and Council Tax Benefit are not taxable.

Who qualifies for Housing Benefit?

You may get Housing Benefit if you are responsible for paying rent and you fulfil the conditions outlined above. Benefit is available to council, housing association and private tenants and to people in the following circumstances:

Boarders and people living in hostels may get Housing Benefit for the accommodation part of their charges.

People living in a houseboat may get benefit for the mooring charges even if they own the houseboat.

People living in a caravan or mobile home may get help with the site charges even if they own the caravan or mobile home.

Joint tenants may receive Housing Benefit towards the part of the costs for which they are responsible.

People living with a landlord who is a close relative may claim Housing Benefit if they live separately in self-contained accommodation. However, they cannot claim benefit if they are part of the same household, or if it is not a 'commercial arrangement'. Get advice if you are unsure about your position.

Who qualifies for Council Tax Benefit?

There are two types of Council Tax Benefit – 'main Council Tax Benefit' and 'second adult rebate'. If you are responsible for paying the Council Tax, you may be able to receive main Council Tax Benefit provided that you fulfil the conditions outlined above. If you are jointly responsible for a bill with someone other than your partner, you can apply for help with your share of the tax.

The second adult rebate may be available to some people, regardless of their income and savings, who have one or more people with low incomes living with them. This is covered on pages 79–80, while the rest of this section covers the main benefit scheme.

How to work out your benefit

Housing Benefit and Council Tax Benefit are worked out using similar calculations. The rules outlined below apply to both benefits unless stated otherwise. The assessment of income and savings and some other aspects of the rules for people aged 60 and over changed in October 2003 with the introduction of Pension Credit. The rules for working out Housing Benefit, Council Tax Benefit and Pension Credit are broadly similar but there are some differences.

To work out how much benefit you will get, follow the steps listed, which are then explained:

1   Calculate the maximum weekly rent and Council Tax for which you can get benefit.
2   Deduct an amount for non-dependants living in your home.
3   Add up the value of your savings, but note that certain types of savings are ignored.
4   Add up your weekly income, but note that certain kinds of income are ignored.
5   Work out the amount the Government says you need to live on, called the 'applicable amount'.
6   Calculate your benefit according to the formula explained below.
7   For Housing Benefit, check that the benefit is above the minimum amount payable, which is 50p a week. There is no minimum payment for Council Tax Benefit.

● **If you are receiving the Pension Credit guarantee credit, you do not need to work out your savings, income and applicable amount as you will receive the maximum eligible benefit minus any deductions for non-dependents.**

1 Your rent and Council Tax

For Housing Benefit purposes, rent is the payment made to occupy your home. It also covers certain service charges – for example for furniture, cleaning communal areas, portering, entry phones, caretakers, rubbish removal. Since April 2003 other support services, such as wardens and community alarms, are now funded separately through a system called 'Supporting People'. Local authorities receive a grant for funding support services including those provided by wardens in retirement (sheltered) housing. (See page 122 for how you get help with your support services.)

You cannot get benefit for water rates and sewerage charges. Homeowners cannot get Housing Benefit; however, they may get help with mortgage interest payments and certain other housing costs from Pension Credit or income-based Jobseeker's Allowance (see pages 53–55).

The maximum Housing Benefit you can get is 100 per cent of your rent including the service charges described above. However, the level of rent on which benefit is calculated may be reduced, as explained below.

High rents

If the local authority considers that your rent is too high or your accommodation is larger than you need (taking into account your circumstances) or that the rent has increased unreasonably while you have been getting Housing Benefit, it may restrict the amount of Housing Benefit.

In addition, some private tenants may face further benefit restrictions if their rent is higher than the typical rent for similar accommodation in the area. These restrictions will not apply to people who were already receiving benefit before 2 January 1996 and have not moved since. Occasionally these rules might also apply to housing association tenants. Before taking up a tenancy, you can ask the local authority for a 'pre-tenancy determination', which will tell you how much of the rent would be eligible for Housing Benefit. Local authorities can make 'discretionary housing payments' if you need help with your rent or

Council Tax. So if your benefit is restricted, you may want to apply for help under this scheme.

If you want to challenge a decision about your benefit or to ask the local authority to use its discretion, it is a good idea to get advice from a local agency. The rules on rent restrictions are complicated and are only covered briefly here. If you need more information, contact Age Concern or consult a book such as the *Welfare Benefits and Tax Credits Handbook* (see page 181).

The Government has started to pilot a new scheme for private tenants in some areas where benefit is based on standard levels of rent and not the actual rent. No-one should receive less benefit and some people, who live in property where the rent is lower than the standard rent, will gain because they will be able to keep the difference.

Council Tax

The maximum Council Tax Benefit you can get is 100 per cent of your bill. From April 1998 to April 2004 benefit was restricted for new claimants who lived in properties in bands F, G and H. However, the Government announced that from April 2004 these restrictions will no longer apply, so the maximum Council Tax Benefit is now 100 per cent for all properties.

Council Tax Benefit is based on the amount you are asked to pay after any 'discounts' or 'reductions' (see pages 149–150) have been given. For example, if you live alone you will receive a 25 per cent discount on your bill, and your benefit will be worked out after this has been deducted.

● **Note that the calculations in this section are all done on a weekly basis. So if you pay your Council Tax in ten monthly instalments, you will first have to work out how much this would be per week over the whole year.**

Heating charges

Some people have a charge for heating included in their rent. You cannot get Housing Benefit for heating and other fuel charges. If, for example, you pay £45 a week rent and £5 of that is for heating, you will only get a maximum of £40 Housing Benefit, as the charge for fuel will be deducted.

If your weekly fuel charges are not stated as a separate amount, the council will deduct the amounts listed as follows:

Heating	£9.80
Hot water	£1.20
Cooking	£1.20
Lighting	£0.80
All fuel	£13.00

The amounts are lower if you occupy only one room.

2 Deductions for non-dependants living in your home

A deduction will normally be made from both your Housing Benefit and your Council Tax Benefit if you have someone else living with you who is not your partner or a dependent child nor a joint tenant or joint owner. This is because people such as grown-up sons and daughters (called 'non-dependants') are expected to contribute to housing costs. However, no deduction will be made if you or your partner are blind or receives Attendance Allowance or the care component of Disability Living Allowance. There are also some types of non-dependant who do not give rise to a deduction – for example, students.

If the person living with you is aged 18 or over, works 16 hours a week or more, does not receive Pension Credit and has a gross income of at least £97 a week, the rates of deduction are as follows:

Gross income of non-dependant	Weekly deduction from rent	Weekly deduction from Council Tax
£97.00 to £143.99	£17.00	£2.30
£144.00 to £185.99	£23.35	£4.60
£186.00 to £246.99	£38.20	£4.60
£247.00 to £307.99	£43.50	£5.80
£308 or more	£47.75	£6.95

If the person who lives with you receives Income Support or income-based Jobseeker's Allowance (JSA), there will be no deduction from your Housing Benefit if they are under 25 and a £7.40 deduction if they are aged 25 or over or receiving Pension Credit. There will be a £7.40 deduction from your Housing Benefit for anyone else who is aged 18 or over and does not fall into any of the categories already mentioned.

For Council Tax Benefit there is no deduction for a non-dependant receiving Pension Credit, Income Support or income-based JSA, while for others aged 18 or over not covered above there will be a £2.30 deduction.

Only one deduction is made for a non-dependent couple living with you.

If you are 65 or over, changes due to non-dependants that would reduce your benefit should not apply until 26 weeks after the change of circumstances.

3 Your savings

Throughout this book the term 'savings' is used to cover savings, capital, investments and property.

If your savings are more than £16,000, you cannot normally get Housing Benefit or the main Council Tax Benefit. However, if you are receiving the guarantee part of the Pension Credit there is no savings limit. For a couple, savings are added together, but the limit is the same. If you are aged 60 or over you can have up to £6,000 in savings without it affecting your benefit. For a couple at least one partner must be aged 60 or over.

If you are not receiving Pension Credit guarantee credit and have savings of between £6,000 and £16,000, an income of £1 a week for every £500 (or part of £500) over £6,000 will be taken into account in working out your benefit. For example, if you have savings of £7,480, you will be treated as having an income of £3 a week. Savings of £10,760 will be treated as £10 a week. This is called 'tariff income'. Savings of £6,000 or less will not affect your benefit.

Savings and capital are normally valued at their current market or surrender value. If there are expenses involved in selling them, 10 per cent will be deducted. Most forms of savings and capital will be taken into account, including:

- cash;
- bank and building society accounts (including current accounts that do not pay interest);
- National Savings accounts and certificates (valued according to rules which the local authority will explain);
- premium bonds;
- income bonds;
- stocks and shares;
- property (other than your home); and
- a share of any savings you own jointly with other people – these will normally be divided equally by the number of joint owners to calculate your share (get advice if you need to value your share of jointly-owned property).

Some types of savings will be ignored, including:

- the value of your home if you own it and are living there;

- the surrender value of a life assurance policy (although if a policy is cashed in the money you receive will normally be counted);
- arrears of certain benefits such as Attendance Allowance, Disability Living Allowance or Income Support for 52 weeks from the date you receive them (or longer if the arrears are £5,000 or over and due to an official error);
- your personal possessions; and
- the £10,000 ex-gratia payment for Far Eastern Prisoners of War (see pages 116–117).

There are also other forms of savings not listed here which are ignored and there are circumstances when property or savings will not be taken into account for a certain period of time – contact the council or an advice agency for more information.

Your money should not normally be counted as both 'income' and 'savings'. So if, for example, your pension is paid four-weekly into a bank account, this should not be assessed as part of your savings unless it is still unspent at the end of the four-week period.

Deprivation of capital (notional capital)

If you 'deprive' yourself of savings in order to get benefit or to increase the amount of benefit, you will be treated as still having those savings. This is known as 'notional capital'. This might occur if you give money to your family or buy expensive items in order to gain benefit. However, you should not be assessed as having notional capital if you have paid off debts or if your spending was 'reasonable' in your circumstances. You should seek advice if you are refused benefit because of notional capital.

4 Your income

This section lists the main types of income that are counted and the main types of income, or parts of income, that are ignored when working out Housing and Council Tax Benefit for people aged 60 and over. If you have any income from other sources you will need to check whether or not they are included. Income is assessed after tax and NI contributions have been paid. For a couple, the income of both partners is added together.

Income that is taken into account includes:

- State Pensions;
- occupational and personal pensions;
- the savings credit part of Pension Credit if you are not receiving the guarantee credit;
- income from annuities;
- most social security benefits (but see below for some exceptions);
- earnings (but see below for amounts ignored);
- Working Tax Credit;
- income from boarders or sub-tenants (but see below for parts ignored);
- maintenance payments from a spouse or former spouse; and
- assumed income from savings over £6,000.

Income that will be fully ignored includes:

- Pension Credit guarantee credit;
- Attendance Allowance;
- Disability Living Allowance;
- actual interest or income from savings or capital of £16,000 or less (only tariff income will be counted, as explained above). Interest is not counted as income but once it is paid into an account it will be counted as part of your savings;
- the special War Widow's Pension for 'pre-1973 widows', which is now £62.68 (in addition to the £10 of a War Widow/Widower's Pension outlined below);

- voluntary or charitable payments – for example money given to you by a charity, family or friends (under the system in place before October 2003 these could reduce your benefit in some circumstances); and
- payments from some forms of equity release schemes which provide an income not based on an annuity.

The following are examples of parts of weekly income that will also be ignored:

- £5 of your earnings if you work and are single;
- £10 of your or your partner's earnings from work;
- £20 of earnings if you work and you are a carer receiving the carer premium or in certain circumstances when you or your partner is disabled (instead of the £5 or £10 listed above);
- £10 of a War Widow/Widower's Pension or War Disablement Pension (the local authority has the discretion to increase the amount from these pensions that is ignored when working out your benefit, but not all authorities operate such schemes: contact your local authority for more information); and
- £20 of any payment from a sub-tenant or boarder and, in the case of a boarder, half of any payment over £20.

To work out your benefit, decide what kinds of income will be ignored and add up the remainder (including tariff income for savings between £6,000 and £16,000).

5 Your applicable amount

This is the weekly amount that is compared with your income to calculate your Housing and Council Tax Benefit. If your income is higher than this, you may still get some help with rent and the Council Tax.

The basic personal allowances for people aged 60 or over are:

Single person aged 60-64	£105.45
Couple, one or both 60-64, both under 65	£160.95
Single person aged 65 or over	£121.00
Couple, one or both aged 65 or over	£181.20

In addition to these basic amounts some people will be entitled to a severe disability premium or a carer premium (or sometimes both). The rules for these are the same as for the additions in Pension Credit and are described on pages 47–49.

For people aged 60–64 the applicable amount is the same as the 'appropriate amount' in Pension Credit. For people aged 65 and over the amount is higher. This was to ensure that at the point of change from Income Support to Pension Credit everyone gained the full amount of savings credit and no-one lost Housing or Council Tax Benefit. However, if you are already receiving the higher levels of Housing Benefit and/or Council Tax Benefit for people aged 65 and over and you apply for Pension Credit, if you are not entitled to guarantee credit, the savings credit will be taken into account and will reduce your benefit

6 Calculating Housing Benefit and Council Tax Benefit

Once you have worked out your applicable amount, compare this figure with your income, including any tariff income from savings over £6,000. If your income is the same as or less than your applicable amount, you will normally get all your rent and Council Tax paid (unless, for example, there are deductions for ineligible service charges, for other people living in your home or because your rent is considered too high). If you are not already receiving Pension Credit then you should be entitled to it, so you should apply.

If your income is more than your applicable amount, the maximum benefit you can get is reduced. You first work out the difference between your income and your applicable amount. The maximum Housing Benefit payable is reduced by 65 per cent of this difference. The maximum Council Tax Benefit is reduced by 20 per cent of the difference.

Another way of explaining the calculation is to say that your maximum Housing Benefit is reduced by 65p for every pound that your income is more than your applicable amount. Your maximum Council Tax Benefit is reduced by 20p for every pound that your income is more than your applicable amount.

Example

Julie Walker is aged 64 and lives alone. Her income consists of a State Pension (Basic and Additional Pension) of £94 a week. She has £2,000 savings and pays £50 a week in rent and £10 a week in Council Tax (after the 25 per cent discount because she lives alone).

The maximum Housing Benefit she can get is £50 a week (100 per cent of her rent). The maximum Council Tax Benefit she can get is £10 a week (100 per cent of her Council Tax). There are no non-dependant deductions because she lives alone.

Her savings will not affect her benefit as they are less than £6,000.

Julie's applicable amount is the standard personal allowance for someone aged 60–64 (£105.45).

Her income is less than her applicable amount, so she will get the maximum Housing Benefit of £50 a week for rent and the maximum Council Tax Benefit of £10 a week. She will also qualify for Pension Credit guarantee credit and should make a claim.

Example

Amir and Samina Khan are both aged 68 and live in a rented house. Amir receives Attendance Allowance and Samina cares for him. She applied for Carer's Allowance and although she satisfied the caring conditions she cannot be paid it because she is receiving a State Pension worth more than the allowance. However, this means that she has an 'underlying entitlement' to Carer's Allowance, so she qualifies for the carer premium. They pay £58 a week in rent. Their Council Tax is £16 a week. They have a State Pension of £127.25 a week, Amir's occupational pension of £66.80 a week, Pension Credit savings credit of £12.40 a week and have savings of £11,700.

The maximum Housing Benefit they can get is £58. The maximum Council Tax Benefit they can get is £16. They have nobody else living with them so there will be no non-dependant deductions.

Amir and Samina add up their income

State Pension	£127.25
Occupational pension	£66.80
Tariff income (for savings over £6,000)	£12.00
Pension Credit savings credit	£12.40
Total	£218.45

They calculate their applicable amount

Personal allowance	£181.20
Carer premium	£25.55
Total	£206.75

Their income is more than their applicable amount, the difference being £11.70 (£218.45 – £206.75).

Their weekly benefit is worked out in the following way:

Rent

100% of rent	£58.00
Less 65% of difference	
(65% of £11.70)	£7.60
Housing Benefit	£50.40

Council Tax

100% of tax	£16.00
Less 20% of difference	
(20% of £11.70)	£2.34
Council Tax Benefit	£13.66

Total benefit is

Housing Benefit	£50.40
Council Tax Benefit	£13.66

Amir and Samina will have to pay £7.60 a week for rent and £2.34 towards the Council Tax.

Example

George and Anne Jones are both 80 and own their home. Their Council Tax is £20 a week. Their weekly income consists of State Pensions of £127.75 a week, income from an annuity of £57.45, and £40 from an occupational pension. They also have £14,000 savings. They have never claimed benefits before but were worried because they were having to use their savings to pay their Council Tax bill. They asked their local advice agency about Pension Credit. It was explained that at present they would not be entitled to Pension Credit but they were advised to claim Council Tax Benefit.

The maximum Council Tax Benefit they can get is £20. They have nobody else living with them so there will be no non-dependant deductions.

George and Anne add up their income

State Pension	£127.75
Occupational pension	£40.00
Annuity income	£57.45
Tariff income from savings	£16.00
Total	£241.20

Their applicable amount is the basic personal allowance for a couple aged over 65 (£181.20).

Their income is £60 more than their applicable amount.

Their weekly benefit is worked out in the following way:

Council Tax

100% of tax	£20.00
Less 20% of difference	
(20% of £60.00)	£12.00
Council Tax Benefit	£8.00

George and Anne will receive £8.00 a week (£416 over the year) towards their Council Tax.

If their granddaughter who is aged 25 and earning £200 a week comes to live with them, she will be counted as a 'non-dependant' and their benefit will be reduced by £4.60 a week.

Second adult rebate

If you are solely liable to pay the Council Tax, you might get a second adult rebate if one or more people with a low income live with you, regardless of the level of your savings and income. This will usually apply only to people who do not have a partner. You may get a 25 per cent rebate if you are responsible for the Council Tax and you have one or more people receiving Pension Credit, Income Support or income-based Jobseeker's Allowance (JSA) living with you. A 15 per cent rebate is given if the person or people living with you have a joint gross income of less than £144; there is a 7.5 per cent rebate if their income is between £144 and £185.99. In assessing the income of people living with you, no account is taken of Attendance Allowance, Disability Living Allowance or the income of anyone receiving Pension Credit, Income Support or income-based JSA.

Example

Janice Grant is a widow who owns her own home. Her son is living with her and receives income-based JSA. Her Council Tax bill for the year is £800. She is not entitled to the main Council Tax Benefit because she has £18,000 savings. However, she applies for a rebate and receives the second adult rebate of 25 per cent (£200) because her son receives income-based JSA.

Some people will be entitled to the main Council Tax Benefit and the second adult rebate. In this case the local authority will award you whichever benefit will give you the greater amount.

Only brief details have been given here as this system can be complicated, so contact the council or a local advice agency if you need further information.

Benefit for people in different circumstances

Absence from home

If you go into hospital on a temporary basis, you can continue to get Housing Benefit and Council Tax Benefit for up to 52 weeks (provided that you intend to return home). If you are temporarily away from home for other reasons, benefit will be paid for up to 13 weeks or up to 52 weeks depending on the reason for your absence. Contact the council or a local advice agency if you need more information about this. You cannot get benefit if you sub-let your home while you are away.

Benefit for two homes

You can normally only get Housing Benefit for one home. However, there are some circumstances in which payments may be made for two homes. For example, you may qualify for benefit on two homes for up to four weeks if you have moved to a new home and it is reasonable that you could not avoid liability to make payments for both homes. Another example is where your move to a new home has been delayed because it was being adapted to meet disability needs. Entitlement to Housing Benefit for two homes is not automatic, so ask your local authority whether you qualify.

Council Tax Benefit is payable only for the home in which you normally live. It is not payable for second homes.

Discretionary housing payments

You can apply to the local authority for an extra payment towards your rent and Council Tax if you are having difficulty meeting your bills. Your local authority will tell you how to make a claim and you will be able to give reasons why you need additional support.

How to claim

If you are claiming Pension Credit, you should also be asked if you want to apply for Housing Benefit and Council Tax Benefit and be given the forms. After any entitlement to Pension Credit has been worked out, the local authority will be notified so that it can calculate your Housing Benefit and Council Tax Benefit.

If you are not claiming Pension Credit, you claim Housing Benefit and Council Tax Benefit directly from your local authority (council).

If you are a couple, only one of you should claim for benefit – it does not matter if the bill is sent in joint names or just to one of you. Your benefit will be calculated on the basis of your combined income and savings.

Before the local authority can work out how much to pay, it may require evidence such as details of your income, savings and the amount of rent you pay. If you have also applied for Pension Credit the local authority will not ask you for information about your income and savings because this information will be passed on from The Pension Service. The normal rule is that Housing Benefit and Council Tax Benefit can be backdated for up to 52 weeks if you can show that you have a good reason for claiming late. However, in the year after the introduction of the Pension Credit (6 October 2003 to 5 October 2004) a claim from someone aged 60 or over can be backdated to 6 October 2003 (without the need to give reasons for a late claim) as long as they have satisfied the conditions since then.

If your circumstances change

If you are not receiving Pension Credit, you must report any changes that might affect your benefit to the local authority. If you are receiving Pension Credit, then whether you need to tell the local authority about changes will depend on the nature of the change and which part of Pension Credit you are receiving. For example, if you are receiving Pension Credit guarantee credit,then you will not need to report changes in your income and savings to the local authority. You may need to report these changes to The Pension Service depending on whether or not you have an assessed income period (see page 62). If you are receiving the savings credit but not the guarantee credit, then there are some changes you must tell the local authority about. These include an increase in your savings to over £16,000, regardless of whether or not you have a Pension Credit assessed income period.

Your local authority will give you information about when you need to let them know if your circumstances change. If you are unsure, contact them to check or otherwise you could have to repay money you have been overpaid or receive less benefit than you are entitled to.

Delays and administrative problems

The local authority should let you know within 14 days of your claim whether you qualify for help (as long as you have provided any information and evidence needed). However, this sometimes takes much longer and in some areas there are problems with the administration of benefit. If you are suffering hardship because the local authority has not yet worked out your claim for benefit or you are having problems with your benefit, contact your nearest Citizens Advice Bureau or a local advice centre for help.

How it is paid

For council tenants, Housing Benefit is usually paid by reducing the rent. If you are a private or housing association tenant, your Housing Benefit may be paid to you by cheque or into a bank account or direct to your landlord.

Most people will pay the Council Tax direct to their local authority, so when you claim benefit your bill will be reduced accordingly. Where this is not possible because, for example, you have already paid the whole bill, the local authority may send you a refund or credit your account.

Overpayment

If you are paid too much benefit, this is known as an overpayment and in most circumstances the local authority can ask you to repay this money. However, an overpayment cannot normally be recovered if it was caused by an 'official error' and you could not reasonably be expected to have known you were being overpaid at the time. Even if the local authority can recover the benefit, it does have some discretion about whether to do so. It is a good idea to seek further advice if you are being asked to repay benefit.

If you disagree with a decision

If you disagree with a decision about your Housing Benefit or Council Tax Benefit, you can ask for the decision to be revised or appeal to an independent tribunal (see pages 32–36).

THE SOCIAL FUND

The Social Fund provides lump-sum payments for expenses which are difficult to meet from low income. There are Funeral Payments, which are described on pages 164–165, and Cold Weather Payments, which are explained on page 144. In addition there are Winter Fuel Payments which are not related to income (see pages 142–143). If you have other expenses – for example if you need a cooker or bedding – you may get help from the discretionary Social Fund in the form of Community Care Grants, Budgeting Loans or Crisis Loans, which are covered in this section.

The payments described here are different from most other social security benefits in that they are discretionary, and Budgeting Loans and Crisis Loans have to be repaid. There is a limited budget for the discretionary Social Fund which restricts the overall amount that can be awarded in grants and loans in any financial year. There is a legal framework for the system and Social Fund decision makers have to follow legal rules called 'directions' and take account of guidance which helps them make decisions. For Community Care Grants and Crisis Loans they must consider all the individual circumstances of the people who apply and decide which applications can be met from the budget. Awards of Budgeting Loans are more 'fact-based', as explained below, rather than being wholly discretionary, but they must still be made from a fixed budget.

The £1,000 capital limit for Social Fund payments described here applies only to people aged 60 or over. For younger people, a capital limit of £500 applies.

Community Care Grants

These are available to people on Pension Credit, Income Support and income-based Jobseeker's Allowance, and to people who will be discharged from care within six weeks and are likely to receive these benefits on discharge. The grants do not have to be repaid. The amount of any savings you have over £1,000 (£500 for people under 60) will be deducted from any grant awarded. For example, if you have £1,100 savings and you need an item costing £300 you would only receive a grant for £200. If you are not sure whether you will get help, you have nothing to lose by applying. It is important to include all the relevant information (see below on 'How to apply').

Grants are available for certain purposes including:

- help with moving out of institutional or residential care (eg for a bed, a cooker, fuel connection or removal costs);
- help to enable you to remain living at home (eg for minor house repairs, bedding and essential furniture or removal costs to more suitable accommodation);

- help with exceptional pressures on families (eg caused by disability, chronic sickness or a breakdown in a relationship); and
- help with certain travel expenses (eg for visiting someone who is ill or attending a relative's funeral).

For details of the other purposes for which grants can be paid, see social security leaflet SB16 *A Guide to the Social Fund*.

Budgeting Loans

These are available to people who have been receiving Pension Credit, Income Support or income-based Jobseeker's Allowance for at least 26 weeks. They enable people to spread the cost of one-off expenses over a longer period. The loans, which are interest-free, have to be repaid, and the amount of any savings over £1,000 (£500 for people under 60) will reduce the amount of the loan.

The applications for Budgeting Loans and Community Care Grants are separate. Therefore you should consider whether you might qualify for a grant before applying for a Budgeting Loan.

You may be able to get a Budgeting Loan for items such as furniture and household equipment, clothing and footwear, removal costs or home improvements or maintenance. In deciding whether you can be awarded a loan, the Social Fund decision maker will look at the time you have been on benefit, the people in your household and any loans you have already had from the Social Fund.

Crisis Loans

These interest-free loans are available to anyone (not just people on benefits such as Pension Credit) who needs something urgently in an emergency or as a result of a disaster (eg fire or flood). The Social Fund decision maker will take into account any family savings or income which is available to you. You may be able to get a loan, provided that this is the only way of preventing serious damage or risk to your health or safety or that of a member of your family.

Repayment of loans

Budgeting or Crisis Loans will be awarded only if the officer thinks you will be able to repay them. Loan repayments will normally be deducted from your benefit and have to be repaid within 78 weeks. In special circumstances the repayment period may be extended further.

The repayment rates will be fixed after taking into account your income and your existing commitments. In the case of Crisis Loans, repayments will not normally begin until after the period of crisis is over.

If you take out a further loan from the Social Fund whilst still repaying an earlier loan, repayment of the further loan will not begin until the original loan has been repaid.

The repayment of loans can be rescheduled if you are having difficulty paying the original rate of repayment. If you are having difficulties, contact your social security office to discuss the level of repayment.

How to apply

To apply for a Community Care Grant you will need form SF300 and for a Budgeting Loan you need application form SF500 from your social security office. If you need a Crisis Loan, ask at the office for an application form SF401. As The Pension Service does not generally have permanent local offices, you should go to the local Jobcentre Plus office to apply for a Crisis Loan, or you may be able to apply by telephone.

When applying for a Community Care Grant or Crisis Loan, you should give as much information as possible about your circumstances and why you need help (eg health problems). If there is not enough room on the form, use a separate sheet.

A local advice agency or Citizens Advice Bureau may be able to help you with the application. You may also wish to include a letter of support from your GP or social worker.

If you are unhappy about a decision

Community Care Grants and loans from the Social Fund are discretionary payments. If you disagree with a decision, you cannot appeal to an appeal tribunal, but instead there is a special system of review. Any request for a review must be made in writing. The first stage of review is at the local office, and you are given the chance to put your case personally to a Social Fund Reviewing Officer. This can be done in person at your local social security office or over the telephone if you prefer. If you are still dissatisfied, you can take your case to the Independent Review Service where it will be considered by a Social Fund Inspector, who is independent of your local social security office. A local advice agency may be able to help if you want to ask for a review.

See social security leaflet GL18 *Help From the Social Fund* or detailed guide SB16 for more information about the Social Fund.

DISABILITY BENEFITS AND PAYING FOR CARE

This part of *Your Rights* describes the main Department for Work and Pensions benefits available to people with disabilities and those who look after them.

Disability Living Allowance and Attendance Allowance are intended to help with the extra costs associated with disability, while other benefits such as Incapacity Benefit and Carer's Allowance are paid to people who are unable to work or who can work only to a limited extent because of their disability or because they are a carer.

There is also a section about paying for care – either in your own home or in a care home – which includes information about local authority charging procedures and financial support.

ATTENDANCE ALLOWANCE AND DISABILITY LIVING ALLOWANCE

Attendance Allowance and Disability Living Allowance (DLA) are intended to provide help towards the extra costs arising from illness or disability. You can claim either Attendance Allowance or DLA. Which one you claim depends on your age.

To qualify for DLA you must need help with personal care, or need supervision, or need help preparing a main meal, and/or have difficulty getting around, and you must claim before your 65th birthday. If you are 65 or over, you should claim Attendance Allowance instead.

This section covers first the conditions for Attendance Allowance and then the conditions for Disability Living Allowance; the third part gives information that applies to both allowances.

Attendance Allowance

This is a benefit for people aged 65 or over who need help with personal care, or need supervision by day, or need someone to watch over them by night, because of physical or mental illness or disability. It does not depend on National Insurance (NI) contributions, is not affected by savings or income, and is paid on top of other benefits or pensions received. Attendance Allowance is not taxable.

There are two weekly rates:

Higher rate £58.80
Lower rate £39.35

Who qualifies for Attendance Allowance?

To qualify for Attendance Allowance you must fulfil all the following conditions:

- You are aged 65 or older.
- You meet the day and/or night conditions described below.
- You must also normally have satisfied the disability conditions for at least six months, but there are 'special rules' for people who are terminally ill, as explained on pages 100–101.
- You are normally resident in the UK when you make your claim, and (unless you are applying under the special rules for terminally ill people) have been here for at least 26 weeks of the last 12 months.

You will receive the lower rate if you fulfil either the day or the night conditions. You will get the higher rate if you fulfil both day and night conditions.

You can receive the allowance if you live alone or with other people and regardless of whether or not you receive any help from someone else – what matters is that you need help with personal care, supervision or watching over, not whether you are actually getting help. You do not have to spend the allowance on paying for care: it is up to you how you use it. However, your local authority may take it into account when assessing whether, and how much, you need to pay for any care services you have.

Day conditions

You can get the allowance if you are so disabled that you require frequent help throughout the day with your normal 'bodily functions' such as eating, getting in or out of bed, going to the toilet or washing. 'Seeing' and 'hearing' are considered bodily functions. For example, if you are visually impaired and need guidance when walking or someone to read your mail, or if you are deaf and need help with communicating, this could help you satisfy the requirement for needing 'frequent help'. You can also get the allowance if you need continual supervision throughout the day to avoid putting yourself or others in substantial danger.

Night conditions

You can also get the allowance if you are so disabled that you require prolonged (periods of at least 20 minutes) or repeated (at least twice nightly) attention during the night to help you with your bodily functions – for example, going to the toilet and getting in and out of bed. You can also get the allowance if another person needs to be awake for a prolonged period or at frequent intervals at night in order to watch over you to avoid putting yourself or others in substantial danger.

The next section covers the qualifying conditions for Disability Living Allowance. You should turn to pages 97–102 for information that covers both allowances, such as how to make a claim and what happens if you are away from home.

Disability Living Allowance

This benefit is for people who become ill or disabled and make a claim before the age of 65, and who:

■ need help with personal care, or need supervision by day, or need someone to watch over them at night; or
■ are unable to walk, have great difficulty walking, or need someone with them when walking in unfamiliar places outdoors; or
■ need help with both of these.

Disability Living Allowance (DLA) does not depend on NI contributions, is not affected by savings or income, and is paid on top of other benefits or pensions received. DLA is not taxable.

There are two parts to DLA: the 'care component', which is paid at one of three rates; and the 'mobility component', which has two different levels. The weekly rates are:

DLA care component		*DLA mobility component*	
Highest rate	£58.80	Higher rate	£41.05
Middle rate	£39.35	Lower rate	£15.55
Lowest rate	£15.55		

Who qualifies for DLA?

To qualify for DLA you must fulfil all the following conditions:

- You meet one or more of the care or mobility conditions described below.
- You are aged under 65.
- You must also normally have satisfied the disability conditions for at least three months, and be expected to satisfy them for at least the next six months, but there are 'special rules' for people who are terminally ill, as explained on pages 100–101.
- You are normally resident in the UK when you make your claim, and (unless you are applying under the special rules for terminally ill people) have been here for at least 26 weeks of the last 12 months.

Although you must have become disabled, and made a claim, before the age of 65, once you are awarded the allowance it will continue, without an age limit, as long as you satisfy either the care or the mobility conditions. If you are receiving the lower or middle rate of the care component and your care needs change, you may be able to qualify for a higher rate after six months. You cannot normally start to receive the lower care component or a mobility component after the age of 65. However, you may be able to receive it if you are already getting one of the components and you can show that you met the conditions for the other component before the age of 65. Seek advice if you think that this may apply to you.

The care component

The care component of DLA is for people who need help with personal care, supervision or watching over because of physical or mental illness or disability. It does not matter if you live alone or with other people, or whether or not you receive any help from someone else – what matters is that you need help with personal care, supervision or watching over, not whether you are actually getting help. You do not have to spend the allowance on paying for care: it is up to you how you use it. However, your local authority may take it into account when assessing whether, and how much, you need to pay for any care services you have.

You will receive £15.55 if you fulfil the lower-rate conditions but not the day or night conditions described below. You will receive the middle level if you fulfil either the day or the night conditions. The highest level is for those who fulfil both day and night conditions. You will see that the day and night conditions are the same as those for Attendance Allowance.

Lower-rate conditions

You will fulfil this condition if you need help with 'bodily functions' for a significant portion of the day, either at one single period or a number of times. For example, you might need some help to get up in the morning and go to bed in the evening but manage alone for the rest of the day. You will also fulfil this condition if you could not prepare a main cooked meal for yourself even if you had the ingredients.

Day conditions

You will fulfil this condition if you are so disabled that you require frequent help throughout the day with your normal bodily functions such as eating, getting in or out of bed, going to the toilet or washing. 'Seeing' and 'hearing' are considered bodily functions. For example, if you are visually impaired and need guidance when walking or someone to read your mail, or you are deaf and need help with communicating, this could help you satisfy the requirement for needing 'frequent help'. You can also get the allowance if you need continual supervision throughout the day to avoid putting yourself or others in substantial danger.

Night conditions

You will fulfil this condition if you are so disabled that you require prolonged (periods of at least 20 minutes) or repeated (at least twice nightly) attention during the night to help you with your bodily functions – for example, going to the toilet and getting in and out of bed. You can also get the allowance if another person needs to be awake for a prolonged period or at frequent intervals throughout the night in order to watch over you to avoid putting yourself or others in substantial danger.

The mobility component

Although the mobility component is given to people who need help getting around, you can spend it how you choose. Remember that it is not available to people who become disabled, or make a claim, after the age of 65.

You can receive the higher level if you are unable to walk or have great difficulty in walking because of a physical disability. The higher level is also available to people who are both blind and deaf and need someone with them when outdoors, to all people who have lost both legs at or above the ankle, and to certain severely mentally disabled people who have severe behavioural problems. If you can walk but need someone with you for guidance or supervision, you may be awarded the lower level.

Using a car

If you own a car and get the higher mobility component of DLA, you may not have to pay road tax. If someone drives a car for you, they can also apply for exemption from road tax. You will get details about this and about getting a car through the Motability Scheme when you first get the allowance.

You can also apply to the local authority for a blue badge (formerly an orange badge) which allows parking with some limitations but without charge at meters or where waiting is restricted. Some local authorities make a small charge for issuing the badge.

Examples of people who may receive DLA

Ellen Johnson is 62 and cannot walk very far owing to severe osteo-arthritis in her hips and hands. Although she can manage to care for herself, she finds cooking very difficult because she cannot do tasks such as cutting, lifting and pouring. She applied for DLA and was awarded the higher level of the mobility component and the lowest level of the care component.

Albert Brown is 64 and suffers from dementia. During the day his wife or another relative stays with him all the time because he is very forgetful and sometimes wanders off or turns on the gas without lighting it. He normally sleeps all through the night. His wife applied for DLA on his behalf and he was awarded the middle level of the care component (because he needs supervision during the day) and the lower level of the mobility component because he needs guidance and supervision when outdoors.

Sarah Bloom is 68 and had a severe stroke six months ago which left her unable to walk and needing a lot of help, for example with washing, dressing and eating. Because she is 68 she is too old to claim DLA. She cannot get any help with her mobility needs but she can apply for Attendance Allowance because she needs personal care.

Remember that these are just examples and your situation is probably different. Whether you qualify for DLA, and if so at what level, will depend on your particular circumstances.

Rules covering both Attendance Allowance and Disability Living Allowance

If you are away from home

If you are receiving NHS treatment in a hospital, you cannot start to receive Attendance Allowance or DLA (although you can make a claim and, if you fulfil the conditions, the allowance can be paid when you go home). However, you may receive either of these allowances if you are a private patient paying for the cost of hospital services.

If you are already receiving Attendance Allowance or DLA and you go into hospital, you will be able to continue to receive the allowance for up to four weeks. However, the allowance will stop sooner if your admission is within 28 days of a previous stay in hospital.

Before July 1996, a stay in hospital did not normally affect the mobility component of DLA. Some people in hospital for 12 months or more in July 1996 received transitional protection and can continue to get an amount equivalent to the lower rate of the mobility component.

For information about Attendance Allowance and DLA for people in care homes, see pages 129–130. In general, a holiday abroad does not affect Attendance Allowance or DLA, nor do periods abroad for medical treatment. You should let your social security office know when you intend to go abroad so that payment of the allowance while you are abroad can be considered.

How to claim

You can get the claim pack for Attendance Allowance (AA1) or DLA (DLA1) by: telephoning the Benefit Enquiry Line on 0800 88 22 00; sending off the tear-off slip on leaflet DS702 (Attendance Allowance) or DS704 (DLA); from some local advice agencies; or on the Internet. If the forms are sent to you because you contacted the Benefit Enquiry Line, from a social security office or because you returned leaflet DS702 or DS704, they will be dated. As long as you return the form in the envelope provided within six weeks, your claim, if successful, will start on the day you requested the pack. If you get the claim pack from a local advice agency, this will not normally be dated and the claim will start from the date the form is received at a disability benefits office.

The intention is that people can describe how their disability affects them on the form and that a medical examination will not normally be necessary. In 2003 a shortened Attendance Allowance form was introduced and a new form for DLA is being piloted. Even so the forms are still quite long and you may want to have some assistance. You can get help to fill in the form from a friend or relative or a local advice agency, or you can telephone the Benefits Enquiry Line on Freephone 0800 88 22 00. If it is difficult for you to get out, your social security office may be able to arrange for a visiting officer to call to help you with the form. The Disability Alliance (address on page 177) produces guides to help people claim Attendance Allowance and DLA.

In the new, shorter Attendance Allowance claim form (AA1), sections 1 and 2 have been combined. The current DLA claim form has two sections: Section 1 deals with information about yourself; and Section 2 asks about how your disability or illness affects you.

If you have difficulty completing the claim form and would rather have a medical examination, you can ask for a doctor to visit. When filling in the form, remember that it does not matter if you actually receive any help or not. Be sure to say what activities are difficult or impossible for you to do. For example, you may have to get dressed on your own because there is no one to help you but do explain if it takes a long time or if it is difficult. If you feel that having answered the questions you have not given a good picture of how your disability affects you, add any extra information you think would be helpful. If you have any problems with filling in the form, do ask for help. There is also a space on the form for your doctor or someone else who knows about your circumstances to complete.

If your claim cannot be decided from the information in the form, the DWP may telephone for more information, ask for further information from someone such as your doctor or community nurse, or it may arrange a medical examination.

If an appointment is made for a doctor to visit, you may want a friend or relative to be there at that time. This will be particularly important if you have difficulty making yourself understood. The doctor, who will not be your own doctor but one appointed by the DWP, will probably examine you and ask further questions. It may be useful to make a note beforehand of the things you need to tell the doctor about when you need help or the difficulties you experience.

When to claim

Although you normally need to fulfil the qualifying conditions for three months before you can start getting DLA and six months for Attendance Allowance, if you have only recently become disabled you should still apply as it may take some weeks to deal with your claim. If you are receiving a lower level of one of the allowances but your condition has deteriorated so you might now qualify for a higher level, you can ask for your case to be reconsidered. You will need to satisfy the care or mobility conditions for the higher level for three months (DLA) or six months (Attendance Allowance) before it can be paid.

You should be aware that if you ask for your case to be looked at again, there is a possibility that instead of awarding a higher level your benefit might be stopped or reduced. You may want to seek help from a local advice agency to discuss your position and to ensure that you include all the relevant information if you ask for your benefit to be reconsidered.

Effect on other benefits

Sometimes if you become entitled to Attendance Allowance or DLA this will also enable you to start receiving other benefits, such as Pension Credit, Housing Benefit or Council Tax Benefit, because these benefits can be higher if you are receiving a disability benefit. To ensure that any benefit entitlement is backdated you need to claim these other benefits at the same time as you claim Attendance Allowance or DLA. If you are not sure of your position, get help from a local advice agency.

Terminal illness

People who are terminally ill can claim DLA or Attendance Allowance without the three-month or six-month waiting period. They will be considered to be terminally ill if they have a progressive illness that is likely to limit their life expectancy to six months or less.

To claim ask your doctor for a DS1500 report, which gives details of your condition. If you are sending the DS1500 report with the Attendance Allowance form, make sure that you have ticked the special rules box on page 3 and only complete Parts 9 and 12 of the form. Then send this in the envelope provided. If you are sending the DS1500 report with the DLA form, complete Section 1, ensuring that you have ticked the special rules box on page 16, and send them in the envelope provided. If you are assessed as being terminally ill, you will automatically receive the higher rate of

Attendance Allowance or the highest level of the care component of DLA. However, if you are under the age of 65 and you want to claim the mobility component of DLA, you will need to fill in pages 1–5 of Section 2 and include this with your claim. Claims should be handled within 10–14 days and a medical examination will not normally be necessary.

If you are not sending the DS1500 report with your claim, you will need to complete all parts of the Attendance Allowance or DLA claim forms.

An application can be made by another person on behalf of someone who is terminally ill with or without their knowledge, so it is possible for people to receive an allowance under the special rules without knowing their prognosis.

How it is paid

Attendance Allowance or DLA may be awarded indefinitely or for a set period, in which case it will be reviewed at the end of this time. If your allowance is awarded for a fixed period you should be sent a renewal claim before the end of that period. There is a system of periodic review for DLA which means that you may be sent a questionnaire or receive a visit to check if your needs are still the same.

In the past Attendance Allowance was normally either paid weekly and collected by order book at the Post Office or paid four-weekly in arrears directly into a bank or building society account. However, as explained on pages 15–16, the Government wants to move to a system where most people receive benefits paid into an account through Direct Payment. If you have your allowance paid by Direct Payment you can ask to be paid weekly if you prefer. If you are receiving another benefit or pension, they will normally be paid together. DLA is normally paid four-weekly unless you were getting

Attendance Allowance by weekly order book before April 1992. However, people claiming under the special rules because they are terminally ill can get weekly payments.

If you disagree with a decision

If you disagree with a decision about your allowance, you can ask for the decision to be revised or make an appeal. You will be sent details about how to do this when you receive the decision. It is important to challenge a decision or get advice as quickly as possible because there are time limits for doing so which generally mean that you must take action within one month. See pages 32–36 for more information or look at the *Disability Rights Handbook* which has more detailed information (see page 181).

For Attendance Allowance see social security leaflet DS702 and claim pack AA1. For DLA see social security leaflet DS704 and claim pack DLA1. See also Age Concern Factsheet 34 *Attendance Allowance and Disability Living Allowance*.

CARER'S ALLOWANCE

Carer's Allowance (which used to be called Invalid Care Allowance) is a benefit for people who are unable to work full-time because they are caring for a severely disabled person for at least 35 hours a week. The benefit is not dependent on having paid NI contributions. Carer's Allowance is taxable.

Do note that in some situations the person you care for could lose money if you start to receive Carer's Allowance. This will apply to a disabled person who receives the severe disability premium or addition as part of their Pension Credit, Income Support, Housing

Benefit or Council Tax Benefit. (See pages 47–48 for more information about the severe disability premium/addition.)

The weekly rates are:

Carer	£44.35
Adult dependant	£26.50

The person being cared for must be receiving one of the allowances referred to below, such as Attendance Allowance. They do not have to be a relative and may live separately or with the carer.

Entitlement to Carer's Allowance may continue for up to eight weeks after the death of the person being cared for.

Who qualifies?

To qualify you must spend at least 35 hours a week looking after someone who is receiving Attendance Allowance (higher or lower rate), the care component of Disability Living Allowance (middle or highest level), or Constant Attendance Allowance of £48.10 or more paid with an industrial, war or service pension.

There is no upper age limit for claiming Carer's Allowance, although if you are receiving a State Pension or another benefit you may not receive the allowance on top of this. (Before October 2002 carers had to be under 65 when they first claimed Invalid Care Allowance.)

A claim can be backdated for up to three months. It is important to claim Carer's Allowance even if the person you care for is still waiting to hear if they qualify for Attendance Allowance or DLA. You must also be resident in the UK and have lived here for at least 26 weeks out of the past 12 months.

You cannot get Carer's Allowance if you earn more than £79 a week after the deduction of allowable expenses. The extra £26.50 which can be claimed for a dependent adult will not be paid if that person earns more than £26.50 a week, including any occupational or personal pension. It also may not be paid if they are receiving a State pension or certain other benefits. When calculating the net earnings of the carer or their partner, certain work expenses are deducted.

Overlap with the State Pension and increases to other benefits

If you are already getting £44.35 a week or more from certain other social security benefits or pensions, you may not be able to get Carer's Allowance as well. This is because it 'overlaps' with some benefits including Incapacity Benefit, State Pension and Widow's Pension. If you have a spouse or partner who is claiming an addition to their benefit for you, that addition will be reduced by the amount of Carer's Allowance received.

However, if you have a low income it may still be worth claiming Carer's Allowance even though it may not be paid in addition to your present benefit or pension. Although Carer's Allowance is counted as income if you claim Pension Credit, Income Support, Housing Benefit or Council Tax Benefit, people entitled to Carer's Allowance may be able to get higher rates of these benefits, owing to the 'carer premium' (carer addition in Pension Credit), as explained on page 49.

Example

Olive Zhukova is 62 and looks after her mother who gets Attendance Allowance. Olive has no savings and has a total income of £109.60 (State Pension of £79.60 and an occupational pension of £30 a week). She is not entitled to Pension Credit because her income is more than £105.45 – the basic Pension Credit level for someone over 60.

She applies for Carer's Allowance but, although she satisfies the conditions, it cannot be paid because her State Pension is more than £44.35 – the level of the allowance. However, because she is entitled to Carer's Allowance her Pension Credit rate is now £131.00 – the basic rate of £105.45 plus the carer addition of £25.55. She is now entitled to £21.40 in Pension Credit to bring her pensions of £109.60 up to the Pension Credit rate.

If you are in this situation you should claim Pension Credit at the same time as you claim Carer's Allowance; otherwise you may not get the benefit fully backdated.

Protecting your pension

If you are entitled to Carer's Allowance, NI contributions will be automatically credited to protect your right to a future State Pension unless you have retained the right to pay the married woman's reduced-rate contributions. If you receive another benefit instead and are not working regularly because you are caring for someone, you may get Home Responsibilities Protection (see pages 12–14). Entitlement to Carer's Allowance can also help you build up State Second Pension, as explained on page 20.

Carer's Allowance after State Pension age

If you are receiving Carer's Allowance when you reach State Pension age (currently 60 for women, 65 for men), it will be adjusted to take account of any State Pension you draw. If your pension is £44.35 or more, the allowance will stop. If your pension is less than £44.35, the allowance will be reduced by the amount of pension received. If you are not entitled to a pension or do not claim one, Carer's Allowance may continue.

If you were 65 or over on 28 October 2002 and receiving ICA when the upper age limit for claiming ICA was abolished, you will be able to continue to receive Carer's Allowance even if you are no longer caring. Otherwise the allowance will stop when you are no longer caring or up to eight weeks later if the person you care for dies.

How to claim

To make a claim you will need claim pack DS700. You can get this pack from your local social security office, by ringing the Benefit Enquiry Line on Freephone 0800 88 22 00 or the Carer's Allowance claim pack order line on 01772 899729, or on the Internet from the DWP website (www.dwp.gov.uk) where you can also claim online. Under new rules that are being phased in, if you are under State Pension age you may need to attend an interview with a personal adviser as a condition of receiving benefit. The aim is to look at work options as well as providing information about other help available.

See social security claim pack DS700 or information leaflet SD4 *Caring for Someone?* Carers UK produces information for carers – see page 176 for the address.

STATUTORY SICK PAY

If you are an employee earning at least £79 a week and you are under 65, you will probably be entitled to Statutory Sick Pay (SSP) if you are off sick for at least four days in a row. This can continue for up to 28 weeks and it will be paid by your employer. The weekly rate is £66.15. You may also get sick pay from your employer's own scheme, depending on the terms and conditions. SSP is taxable. Contact your employer for details.

If you are unable to work because of sickness but not entitled to SSP, for example because you are self-employed or unemployed, you may be entitled to Incapacity Benefit, as explained below.

INCAPACITY BENEFIT

This is a benefit for people who are unable to work owing to illness or disability. It was introduced on 13 April 1995 and replaced Sickness Benefit and Invalidity Benefit. It is based on NI contributions (except for some people disabled early in life). It is not generally means-tested but for claims on or after 6 April 2001 a personal or occupational pension of more than £85 a week may reduce benefit, as explained below.

This section mainly covers the current rules for Incapacity Benefit. However, if you were transferred from Invalidity Benefit to Incapacity Benefit in April 1995, you may be covered by transitional rules, as explained on page 111.

There are three levels of Incapacity Benefit. If you are an employee, you will probably be paid Statutory Sick Pay (SSP) by your employer for the first 28 weeks that you are unable to work (see above). However, if you are not entitled to SSP, for example because you are self-employed or unemployed, you may be able to get the short-term lower rate of Incapacity Benefit for up to 28 weeks. The short-term higher rate of Incapacity Benefit is paid from 29 weeks to 52 weeks of incapacity while the long-term rate is paid after 52 weeks. (People who are terminally ill or who receive the highest rate of the care component of Disability Living Allowance (DLA) will receive the long-term rate from 29 weeks.) The long-term rate can continue up to pension age as long as you remain unable to work. The short-term higher rate and the long-term rate are taxable, but the short-term lower rate is not.

The weekly rates of Incapacity Benefit are:

Short-term lower rate (under pension age)	£55.90
Short-term higher rate (under pension age)	£66.15
Long-term rate	£74.15

If you become unable to work before the age of 45, you will receive an age addition which will be paid when you start to receive the long-term rate of Incapacity Benefit. There are two rates, depending on the age at which you become unable to work:

Under 35	£15.55
35–44	£7.80

Who qualifies?

To qualify for Incapacity Benefit you must be assessed as incapable of work and be under State Pension age (currently 60 for women, 65 for men) when your period of incapacity began.

You must normally also satisfy certain NI contribution conditions in the last three tax years; however, there are exceptions to this for certain people disabled before the age of 25.

The incapacity test

For the first 28 weeks of incapacity you will normally only need to provide a medical certificate from your doctor stating that you are unable to do your normal job, if you have one.

After 28 weeks, or from the start of incapacity if you have not worked for 8 out of the 21 weeks prior to your claim, most people will have to undertake a 'personal capability assessment'. This will involve a questionnaire and, in some cases, a medical examination, to decide whether you are incapable of any work – not just your normal job. These processes can begin earlier than the 28th week. However, you will not be subject to the incapacity test if you are terminally ill, receive the highest care component of DLA, are registered blind, have certain severe medical conditions, or in some circumstances when you are entitled to industrial disablement benefit or a war pension.

Increases for a husband or wife

You may be entitled to an increase for an adult dependant if your husband or wife is aged 60 or over (unless you are covered by the transitional rules for people previously receiving Invalidity Benefit). If you are receiving the long-term rate of Incapacity Benefit, the increase for a dependent is £44.35 a week. If you are receiving either of the short-term rates, and you are under pension age, the increase is £34.60.

However, these increases 'overlap' with any State Pension or certain other State benefits that your husband or wife is receiving. So if, for example, your wife had a State Pension of £50 a week, you would not be entitled to an increase for her; if her pension was £20 a week, the amount you could receive would be reduced by £20.

If your husband or wife has earnings of more than £55.65 a week (if you are getting the long-term rate) or £34.60 a week (for the short-term rate), then you cannot receive an adult dependency increase – in this context any occupational or personal pension your spouse receives will be counted as earnings.

Work and Incapacity Benefit

Under the 'permitted work' rules you are able to work for up to 16 hours a week, on average, and earn up to £72 a week for 26 weeks (the figure of £72 may increase during the year). In some cases this can be extended by a further 26 weeks if your adviser at the Jobcentre Plus office agrees that this would help you towards working 16 hours a week or more. After the 26 or 52 weeks you can only work and earn up to £20 a week unless you are in certain types of 'supported permitted work', such as work in a sheltered workshop, when you will be able to continue to earn up to £72 a week. You must tell the social security office that you are working. For more information contact your Jobcentre Plus office.

Occupational and personal pensions

If you make a claim for Incapacity Benefit and you have an occupational, stakeholder or personal pension of more than £85 a week, this will normally reduce your benefit. For every £1 of pension more than £85, you will lose 50 pence of benefit.

A pension will not reduce your benefit if you have been receiving Incapacity Benefit since before 6 April 2001, nor do these rules apply to new claimants in receipt of the highest rate of the care component of Disability Living Allowance.

When you reach State Pension age

The long-term rate of Incapacity Benefit cannot be paid after State Pension age. So once you reach State Pension age (currently 60 for women, 65 for men), you should draw the State Pension. It will be worked out as explained in the section starting on page 2, although if you were receiving an age addition with your Incapacity Benefit this can be paid with your State Pension as an invalidity addition (after the deduction of any Additional Pension and contracted deductions).

If you become incapable of work before State Pension age and are receiving short-term Incapacity Benefit, this can continue until you have been unable to work for up to a year. For people over State

Pension age the short-term lower rate of Incapacity Benefit is £71.15 a week and the higher rate is £74.15, although you may get less if you do not have enough contributions for a full Basic State Pension. You may also receive Additional and Graduated Pension. There is an adult dependency increase of £42.65 which you may receive if your husband or wife is aged 60 or over – depending on any earnings, pensions or other benefits they receive.

How to claim

To claim Incapacity Benefit, contact your local Jobcentre Plus office. Under rules that are being gradually introduced nationally, people claiming Incapacity Benefit (and other benefits for people of working age) will normally be required to attend a work-focussed interview as a condition of benefit. The aim is to look at work options as well as to provide information about what practical and financial help is available. The Government also wants to provide better support and help to enable people receiving Incapacity Benefit to get back to work if they are able to do so. Four pilots started in October 2003 and a further three are planned from April 2004.

If you disagree with a decision

If you disagree with a decision about your benefit, you can ask for the decision to be revised or you can make an appeal, as explained on pages 32–36.

If you were receiving Invalidity Benefit on 12 April 1995

If you were transferred from Invalidity Benefit to Incapacity Benefit in April 1995 and have continued to receive Incapacity Benefit since then (without a break of more than eight weeks, or longer if covered by certain linking rules), you will be covered by the transitional rules. These rules were introduced to provide some protection against changes which could reduce the amount of benefit people received. If you are covered by the transitional rules, your Incapacity Benefit will not be taxable.

If you are covered by transitional rules, the basic rate of Incapacity Benefit is £74.15 (ie the same as the long-term rate for new claimants). The increase for a dependent husband or wife is also the same (£44.35) and this will be reduced by their pensions, benefits or earnings in the same way. However, if you were receiving an increase for a dependent husband or wife with your Invalidity Benefit, this can continue to be paid if your spouse is under 60. If you make a claim for the dependant's increase now, or there is a break of a certain length in entitlement, the rules described on page 109 will apply, which means that your husband or wife must be aged 60 or over.

You may receive Invalidity Allowance if you were previously getting it with your Invalidity Benefit. The rates, which depend on the age at which you became unable to work, are:

Under 40	£15.55
40–49	£10.00
Men 50–59, women 50–54	£5.00

You may also receive an Additional Rate based on any entitlement to Additional State Pension you built up between 1978 and 1991. However, the level of Additional Rate is frozen at the amount you were receiving with your Invalidity Benefit before April 1995 and will not be increased in future years. It also 'overlaps' with Invalidity Allowance, so your Additional Rate will reduce any Invalidity Allowance you are entitled to.

In other respects the Incapacity Benefit rules are generally the same as for new claimants and are described on page 108, although some people who have been incapable of work since before 13 April 1995 are exempt from the personal capability assessment.

SEVERE DISABLEMENT ALLOWANCE

Severe Disablement Allowance (SDA) was abolished for new claimants on 6 April 2001. However, you can still receive it if you were entitled to the benefit on or before 5 April 2001 and have been receiving it continuously since then (although short breaks may be covered by certain linking rules). If you are already in receipt of SDA it can be paid as long as you continue to satisfy the entitlement conditions. It is a benefit for people who are incapable of working but who do not have enough contributions to get Incapacity Benefit.

If you are under State Pension age and become unable to work due to ill health, you may be able to claim Incapacity Benefit if you fulfil the contribution conditions or otherwise may be entitled to help through income-related benefits.

SDA is not based on NI contributions and is not taxable. The basic weekly rates are:

Claimant	£44.80
Adult dependant	£26.65

There are also additions for people who became unable to work before the age of 60; these are added to the basic rate of £44.80. The weekly rates are:

Under 40	£15.55
40–49	£10.00
50–59	£5.00

SDA is not means-tested but is taken into account if you apply for income-related benefits such as Income Support or Pension Credit. Contact a local advice agency or write to Age Concern at the address on page 183 if you need more information about SDA.

If you applied on or after 13 April 1995, you will only have received the adult dependency increase for your husband or wife if they are aged 60 or over. If they have earnings over £55.65 or receive a State pension or benefit of £26.65 or over, you may not be able to get this increase. If you have been receiving the increase since before 13 April 1995 it can continue, even if your husband or wife is under 60.

SDA can continue to be paid after you reach State Pension age but the 'overlapping benefit' rules apply, which means that it is not paid in addition to certain other State benefits or pensions. You cannot receive both the full amount of SDA and a State Pension. If you do not qualify for a State Pension or it is less than SDA, you can continue to receive SDA to make your benefit up to the basic level of £44.80 plus the age addition if you qualify for one. You can continue to receive the allowance instead of drawing your pension.

OTHER BENEFITS FOR PEOPLE WITH DISABILITIES

This section gives brief information about other benefits for people with disabilities. More detailed information is given in the leaflets mentioned or you could look at the *Disability Rights Handbook* (see page 181).

Industrial injuries scheme

The industrial injuries scheme can provide help to people who are disabled as a result of an accident at work or an industrial disease. The main benefit is Disablement Benefit, which can be paid in addition to other National Insurance benefits such as Incapacity Benefit or State Pension. The level of payment depends on how disabled you are assessed as being. If you are awarded Disablement Benefit at the 100 per cent rate, you may also qualify for Constant Attendance Allowance if you need care and attention. There is also an Exceptionally Severe Disablement Allowance for those who are likely to need high levels of attention on a permanent basis.

See social security leaflets SD6 *Ill or Disabled Because of a Disease or Deafness Caused by Work?*, SD7 *Disabled Because of an Accident at Work?*, SD8 *Ill or Disabled Because of Working With Asbestos in Your Job?* and DB1 *A Guide to Industrial Injuries Schemes Benefits*.

War Disablement Pensions and War Widows'/ Widowers' Pensions

You may be entitled to a War Disablement Pension if you are disabled (physically or mentally) as a result of war or peacetime service in HM Armed Forces. The amount awarded depends on how disabled you are. You may get a tax-free lump sum or a pension. Civilians and certain other people, such as those in the Mercantile Marines, are covered by War Pensions for injuries occurring in certain circumstances – time limits may apply. There are extra allowances which may be paid in addition to a War Disablement Pension. These include War Pensions Constant Attendance Allowance for people needing a lot of care and attention because of their pensioned disablement, and a Mobility Supplement if they have difficulty walking because of that disablement.

You may be entitled to a War Widow's/Widower's Pension if you are the widow or widower of someone whose death was due to, or substantially hastened by, service in HM Armed Forces or an injury due to war. The amount paid depends on the rank of the person who has died and the age of the widow or widower.

If you remarry, your War Widow's Pension will be withdrawn. Since 19 July 1995 a war widow who remarried but is widowed again or whose marriage ends in divorce or judicial separation may now claim her pension again. From April 2002 this also applies to a widower's pension. The pension will normally restart from the date you claim. For a claim form or more information, ring the Veterans Helpline (formerly the War Pensions Helpline) on Freephone 0800 169 2277 or write to the Veterans Agency (formerly the War Pensions Agency) (address on page 180).

The Veterans Agency War Pensioners' Welfare Service provides an advice and support service to all war pensioners and war widows/widowers living in the UK. The Welfare Service also gives advice and assistance to anyone who thinks they may be entitled to claim a War Disablement Pension or War Widows'/Widowers' Pension. Contact details of your nearest welfare office can be found in your local telephone directory under 'Veterans Agency' or you can contact the Veterans Agency at the address on page 180.

There are also a number of service organisations which can help war pensioners and war widows/widowers. Details of some of these organisations are included in the leaflet mentioned below.

See Veterans Agency leaflet WPA1.

Ex-gratia payments for British groups held prisoner by the Japanese

In November 2000 the Government announced that it would make a single ex-gratia payment of £10,000 to the surviving members of British groups held prisoner by the Japanese during the Second World War. Payments are made to:

- surviving members of the armed forces or merchant navy who were held prisoner in the Far East;

- certain former service personnel who were members of the colonial forces;

- British civilians interned in the Far East (you need to have been born in the UK or had a parent or grandparent born in the UK); and

- a surviving widow or widower of these groups (provided that they were still married at the time of death).

Payments will not be taken into account for income-related benefits. For more information contact the Veterans Agency at the address on page 180.

PAYING FOR CARE

This section explains the help you can get with paying for the costs of care in all settings. This might be care at home (such as personal care or domestic help in your home, day care or a night sitting service) or care in a care home. It covers people living in England, Scotland and Wales. Although the system in Northern Ireland is broadly similar, there are some differences, so contact Age Concern Northern Ireland if you need more information.

Many people buy their own care without social services' help. This section looks at the help you can receive from social services and how you may be charged for that help. There are national rules for charging for care in care homes but each local authority is able to decide whether and how much to charge for care to help you remain at home, subject to certain minimum requirements.

Applying for help with care

If you need help with your care, either to help you to remain at home or if you think you might need to move into a care home, you can ask for an assessment of your needs by the local authority (the county, metropolitan or London Borough or unitary authority). The social services department (social work department in Scotland) will be responsible for arranging an assessment of your care needs. In some areas in England and Wales, Care Trusts will be taking on the role of assessment. After this assessment it will decide whether it can offer you any help either to enable you to stay at home or in a care home. Each local authority has its own criteria for making these decisions. Some local authorities have a ceiling on the amount (either the number of hours or the cost) of care it will provide to help you remain at home. If you do not agree with its decision, you can make a complaint through the complaints procedure.

In England and Wales your carer (if you have one) is entitled to an assessment in their own right and to services that will help them care for you. They have a right to an assessment even if you do not want to be assessed. In Scotland a carer is entitled to an assessment of their needs which will be taken into account in deciding the services the person being cared for is offered.

See Age Concern Factsheet 41 *Local Authority Assessment for Community Care Services*.

PAYING FOR CARE AT HOME

This section looks at the help you can receive either from local authorities through direct payments or from the Independent Living Fund in paying for care to help you remain at home. It then explains the rules that a local authority uses when working out how much to charge you for care it has provided or arranged for you.

Direct payments

Local authorities can give people cash payments as an alternative to directly arranging community care services. Since April 2003 (June 2003 in Scotland) it has been mandatory for local authorities to offer direct payments to older people who meet the other eligibility requirements. This will also be the case in Wales at some point during 2004.

You can choose to employ a carer yourself, or use a local home care agency if you do not wish to take on the responsibility of being an employer. You may find that there is a support group in your area to help people with managing direct payments. Carers in England and Wales are also able to receive direct payments instead of services which can be provided for them.

To get a direct payment you have to be able to manage the payments, alone or with assistance. (In Scotland people who manage your affairs, such as an attorney or guardian, can have a direct payment.) They cannot usually be used to pay a spouse or close relative in the same household. The local authority has to monitor that the money is being spent on the care you need. If you want a direct payment but your local authority refuses, you can use the complaints procedure.

For more information about direct payments in your area, contact your local authority. In Scotland, call the direct payments helpline on 0131 558 3450. See also Age Concern Factsheet 24 *Direct Payments from Social Services*.

The Independent Living Fund (ILF)

The Independent Living (Extension) Fund makes payments to people already receiving help at the end of March 1993. The Independent

Living (1993) Fund makes payments to applicants since that date. Both provide cash payments to enable severely disabled people to pay for personal care or help with household tasks in order to remain living at home.

You can be considered for help from the discretionary Independent Living (1993) Fund only if you are under the age of 66. You must also be receiving the highest care component of Disability Living Allowance, have no more than £18,500 in savings, be receiving Income Support, income-based JSA or Pension Credit guarantee credit, or not be able to afford the care you need from your income, and be receiving services or cash from the local authority, currently to the value of at least £200 a week. The maximum weekly payment from the ILF is normally £420.

For more information about the Independent Living (1993) Fund, contact your local authority social services department.

Charges for care at home

Each local authority has discretion about whether it will charge people who receive care either provided or arranged by the local authority. Very few authorities do not charge anything. In Scotland personal care is free if you are 65 or over, but you will still be charged for non-personal care services. Any services arranged under Section 117 of the Mental Health Act for aftercare following detention in hospital must be free (however, in Scotland the different laws mean that these services are chargeable if they are not within the definition of personal care). Any services arranged by the NHS, such as visits by the community nurse, are also free. In England and Wales if your care comes under the definition of Intermediate Care (ie to avoid you going to hospital or when you have just come out of hospital), it will be free for six weeks. In Scotland you get free services for four weeks when you come out of hospital (even if some of the care is non-personal care).

However, any charge you do pay must be 'reasonable' for you to pay, and you have the right to ask the local authority to reduce the amount or waive it altogether. It is important that the local authority is aware if you have extra costs because of your disability, such as having to pay for a gardener or someone to clean the house, or taxis because you cannot use public transport, so that they can take account of these costs. Any charge should only be based on your resources. If you disagree with your charge you can use the local authority's complaints procedure.

The Department of Health has issued guidance for England (called *Fairer Charging Policies for Home Care and other non-residential Social Services*) setting out a framework which local authorities must use when they decide their policies. You should be left with at least £131.81 (for a single person aged 60 or over – the figures vary according to your age), and you should only be charged the full cost of the service if your capital (excluding your home) is above £20,000. Some local authorities have set more generous capital limits and/or have set a maximum charge. Any earnings are not taken into account. The local authority should also offer to check that you are getting all the benefits you are entitled to.

The Convention of Scottish Local Authorities (CoSLA) has produced guidance on charging older people for 'non-personal' care services. Guidance on this subject has also been issued in Wales – contact AC Cymru at the address on page 183 for more information.

See Age Concern Factsheet 6 *Finding Help at Home* and Factsheet 46 *Paying for Care and Support at Home*.

Supporting People

Since April 2003 certain support services (such as community alarms or wardens), which were previously funded from a number of sources including Income Support and Housing Benefit, have been funded from a single fund called Supporting People. Supporting People is administered by the local authority and payment is made to the housing provider. If you are a service user who had been assisted with these costs from Income Support or Housing Benefit prior to April 2003, you should not have been left worse off following the changes. If you are a service user who did not previously receive those benefits, you may still be able to claim assistance from the local authority. The local authority may assess eligibility for assistance in such cases using the same *Fairer Charging* policy (see page 121) as for home care, and if it does not already it should be working towards this.

See Age Concern Information Sheet IS19 *Supporting People*, which is available from the Age Concern Information Line on 0800 00 99 66.

Short breaks

If the local authority arranges short periods in a care home, it can charge in one of two ways as long as the stay is less than eight weeks. It can either choose to have a 'set' charge which must be reasonable, or it can use the means test used to calculate the charge for care homes (see below). The value of your home will be ignored as it counts as a temporary stay. If your care break is in hospital, arranged by the NHS or is part of Intermediate Care, it will be free. Benefits may be affected depending on how frequent your care is and how long it lasts.

PAYING FOR CARE IN A CARE HOME

This section summarises the help you can get with care home charges. The term 'care home' covers all homes that are registered homes under the Care Standards Act 2000. This includes independent homes and those owned by the local authority and which provide personal and/or nursing care. Before the local authority can offer any financial help you need to have an assessment of your needs as described on page 118. Please note also that the information in this section does not apply to people whose care is in a home which provides nursing care which has been arranged and fully paid for by the NHS and who are regarded as long-stay NHS patients. An important Health Ombudsman report in February 2003 indicated that there may be more people who should qualify for this full provision. This section also does not apply to those who receive their care free under Section 117 of the Mental Health Act (the rules are different in Scotland).

In England and Wales the NHS is responsible for the funding of care provided by a registered nurse in a care home providing nursing. In England there are three 'bands' (£40, £75.50 or £125 a week), depending on the level of nursing you are assessed as needing (Primary Care Trusts now have the flexibility to agree an amount between £40 per week and the medium band consistent with the nursing needs of the individual concerned). In Wales there is one level of £105. In Scotland local authorities meet £65 towards the cost of nursing care. However, for people aged 65 and over in Scotland your personal care costs are also met (set at £145 a week).

For more information about the level of funding you are likely to receive towards your nursing care, see Age Concern Factsheet 20 *Continuing NHS Health Care, 'Free' Nursing Care and Intermediate Care*, or contact Age Concern England, Scotland or Cymru at the addresses on page 183.

If you need help with your care home costs you can get help from the local authority and you may also get benefits from the Department for Work and Pensions (DWP). In some circumstances Attendance Allowance or Disability Living Allowance (DLA) can be paid, as explained later.

You should be aware that although there are national assessment and charging procedures, sometimes things do not run as smoothly as described here. For example, there may be delays in obtaining an assessment, or the local authority may not agree to take financial responsibility. If you have problems a local advice agency may be able to help.

Care arranged by the local authority

If the local authority agrees to arrange a place for you in a private or voluntary care home, it will be responsible for paying the full fee to the home and assessing your income and savings to work out how much you must pay towards the fees. If you are in a local authority home, the local authority uses the same rules to work out how much you should pay towards the cost of providing the home. If you wish, you will be able to choose a different home (subject to certain conditions). If the home you choose is more expensive than the local authority thinks you need, then the local authority will arrange this as long as there is someone (such as a friend, relative or charity) able to make up the difference. You cannot use your own money to make up the difference, unless you are in the period of the 12 week disregard of the property, or have entered into a deferred payment agreement (see page 127).

If there is no suitable place at the price the local authority would usually pay for someone with your assessed needs, it will be responsible for paying for a more expensive place to meet your needs.

Charging procedures

For the local authority assessment, if you have savings of more than an upper capital limit, you will have to pay the full fee until your savings reach that amount. In England the upper capital limit is £20,000. In Scotland the level is £19,000 and in Wales £20,500. In Scotland if you are 65 or over your full fee is the accommodation and living costs only as the local authority meets the personal care (£145 per week) and nursing costs (£65) of the home. If you are under 65 it just meets the nursing costs.

If you are already in a home and are using up your savings, you should apply to the local authority for help a few months before your savings get down to the capital limit. (See pages 126–127 for how your former home is treated.)

For the local authority assessment, savings of no more than a lower capital limit will be ignored and savings between the upper and lower capital limits will be counted as though you have an additional £1 a week income from every £250 (or part of £250). This is called 'tariff income'. In England the lower capital limit is £12,250. In Wales it is £13,500 and in Scotland £11,750.

In carrying out the assessment the local authority will take into account your income, including any Pension Credit which you are entitled to. Pension Credit is also assessed on your income and savings but the rules are different in some respects. For Pension Credit the first £10,000 of savings are ignored and every £500 (or part of £500) over £10,000 will be assumed to produce an income of £1 a week. If you are aged 60 or over, you may be able to claim Pension Credit guarantee credit whilst you are in the care home. You may also qualify for Pension Credit savings credit if you are aged 65 or over (see pages 55–59). Your appropriate amount will be calculated in the same way as if you were living in ordinary accommodation.

The local authority calculates how much you should contribute towards the cost of your care by looking at your capital and income (including tariff income). The amount which you are asked to contribute should leave you with a Personal Expenses Allowance of at least £18.10 a week in England and Scotland. The rate is slightly higher (£18.40) in Wales. If you have enough qualifying income to receive Pension Credit savings credit, or do not receive this benefit because your qualifying income is too high, you should also be allowed to retain up to £4.65 per week of that income in addition to the Personal Expenses Allowance.

See Age Concern Factsheet 10 *Local Authority Charging Procedures for Care Homes*.

Owning your home

Local authority assessment

If you are in a care home and you own your own home, its value will normally be taken into account, unless your stay is only temporary; or if your partner lives there, a child under 16 for whom you are responsible, or a 'relative' who is either disabled or aged 60 or over lives in the property. In addition, if you have capital of less than the upper capital limit (see page 125) there is a 12-week period when the value of the home will be ignored from the time you become a permanent resident. This is on top of any disregard while your stay was considered temporary.

The local authority can also choose to ignore the value of your home if someone else lives there – for example, a friend aged over 60 or a relative or friend under 60 who has been caring for you for a substantial period. If the local authority says it will not use this discretion, you might want to complain through the formal complaints procedure.

If the local authority does not ignore the value of your former home, it will be able to place a 'charge' on its value, so that it can reclaim money owed to it when the property is sold. You should seek legal advice about this. Local authorities have been given an extra grant to help them offer more legal charges and not to put pressure on residents to sell their homes. Instead you can enter into a 'deferred payment agreement' with the local authority.

For details about who counts as a relative in this situation and further information about the treatment of the former home, see Age Concern Factsheet 38 *Treatment of the Former Home as Capital for People in Care Homes*.

The local authority will also be able to take account of certain assets which you might have transferred to someone else in order to pay less for your care. It may be able to recover any debt from the recipients of such assets if the transfer was made within six months of the local authority arranging the funding of the place in the home. Even if the transfer was made more than six months before, the asset can still be taken into account.

See Age Concern Factsheet 40 *Transfer of Assets and Paying for Care in a Care Home*.

Pension Credit assessment

If you own your own home, its value will normally be taken into account when your savings are assessed for Pension Credit.

However, this value will be ignored for 26 weeks, or longer if reasonable, if you are taking steps to sell it. The value of your home will also be ignored if your spouse or partner lives there, or a 'relative' who is either disabled or aged 60 or over lives in the property.

For details about the system for people in care homes needing local authority support, see Age Concern Factsheet 10 *Local Authority Charging Procedures for Care Homes*.

Couples

When one of a couple enters a care home, the local authority will assess the amount that the resident has to pay towards the fees solely on the resident's income and savings. However, a spouse is considered to be a 'liable relative', which means that they may have an obligation to contribute towards the cost of care. An unmarried partner has no liability under the local authority charging procedures to pay for a partner's care.

The local authority has no power to insist on a means test of your spouse and, although some authorities may have developed their own formulae, there are no specific national rules about how much your spouse must pay. A spouse can be invited to make a contribution, and a voluntary agreement may be reached.

If no voluntary agreement is reached, the local authority can make a complaint to a Magistrates' Court (Sheriff Court in Scotland), which has the power to decide how much, if anything, a liable relative should pay. The Department of Health has announced that it intends to abolish the liable relative rule in the future.

If you have an occupational or personal pension and your spouse is not also living in a care home with you, the local authority will ignore half the pension when assessing your income if you pass at least this amount to your spouse.

The local authority can also use its discretion to vary the amount of the Personal Expenses Allowance. For example, you might want to ask for this to be done if you are not married to your partner, as the local authority will not automatically ignore half of your pension in this situation.

The person at home may be able to claim benefits such as Pension Credit in their own right, depending on their income and savings.

See Age Concern Factsheet 39 *Paying for Care in a Care Home if You Have a Partner*.

Attendance Allowance or Disability Living Allowance in a care home

The mobility component of Disability Living Allowance (DLA) is not affected by admission to a care home.

Whether or not you can receive Attendance Allowance or the care component of DLA will depend on how the fees are being met.

If you are paying the full charges in a care home, you can claim and receive Attendance Allowance or DLA provided you fulfil the other conditions (see pages 90–92 and 93–95). You can receive these allowances whether you arranged the admission yourself or the local authority arranged the admission. Payments for nursing care in a home providing nursing do not affect your ability to receive Attendance Allowance or DLA. In Scotland if the local authority pays for your personal care costs, you cannot receive Attendance Allowance. If the NHS pays for the full fees your Attendance Allowance or DLA will be affected as you will be regarded as a hospital inpatient (see page 97).

If you need local authority financial support in order to meet the home's fees, you cannot start to receive Attendance Allowance or the care component of DLA. If you are already receiving one of these allowances, it will stop four weeks after the admission.

However, you may still retain an 'underlying entitlement' to the allowance, so that if, for example you move out of the home, you could start receiving the allowance again without making a fresh claim. You should contact the social security office and ask for the allowance to be paid again. If the local authority temporarily provides funding but will later be reimbursed in full by you, for example under a deferred payment agreement, Attendance Allowance or the care component of DLA can be paid for that period. Pension Credit can be paid at the same time as Attendance Allowance or the care component of DLA in these circumstances, although it may not be available if you own a house which is not being marketed. Get advice if your Attendance Allowance or DLA has been stopped and you do not think that it should have been.

See Age Concern Information Sheet IS13 *Attendance Allowance in Care Homes*, which is available from the Age Concern Information Line on 0800 00 99 66.

OTHER BENEFITS AND FINANCIAL SUPPORT

This part of *Your Rights* gives details about other benefits and financial help that may be available for older people. It covers Working Tax Credit and benefits for people who are unemployed or bereaved. It then describes other types of financial support and concessions, including help with paying for fuel and other household bills, health costs and travel concessions. There is also information about help with the Council Tax. This includes brief information about the additional £100 payment announced in the Budget for households where someone is aged 70 or over.

WORKING TAX CREDIT

Working Tax Credit and Child Tax Credit were introduced in April 2003. They replaced, and extended, the financial support given through the Disabled Person's Tax Credit, Working Families' Tax Credit and some of the support for children previously provided by the benefit system. Support for children is not covered in this book, so this section just gives brief information about Working Tax Credit for people without dependant children.

Working Tax Credit can be claimed by single people or couples who are employed or self-employed whether they have children or not. There is no upper age limit for making a claim. To qualify for Working Tax Credit you must normally be living in the UK and:

- if you qualify for the 'disability element' or the '50 plus element', you must work for at least 16 hours a week; or
- if you do not qualify for these elements, you must work for at least 30 hours a week.

You may qualify for the disability element if you have a disability which puts you at a disadvantage in getting a job and if you are, or have recently been receiving, one or more of certain incapacity or disability benefits (including Incapacity Benefit, Disability Living Allowance or Attendance Allowance).

You may qualify for the 50 plus element if you are aged 50 or over and you return to work for at least 16 hours a week and, for the six months before you started work, you were getting one or more of certain benefits (including Pension Credit, Jobseeker's Allowance, Incapacity Benefit or Income Support). The 50 plus element is only paid for 12 months.

If you fulfil these criteria, whether you will receive Working Tax Credit, and if so how much, will depend on your circumstances, your income (including that of your partner if you have one) and whether you qualify for the disability or the 50 plus elements.

Working Tax Credit is administered by the Inland Revenue and the assessment of income and savings, and the way the tax credit is administered, is different to the rules for social security benefits.

For more information or a claim form, contact your local Jobcentre Plus office or Inland Revenue Enquiry Centre or ring the Tax Credits Helpline on 0845 300 3900. If you have access to the Internet, you can get more information or claim online at www.inlandrevenue.gov.uk/taxcredits

JOBSEEKER'S ALLOWANCE

Jobseeker's Allowance (JSA) is a taxable benefit for people who are unemployed. There are two elements: contribution-based JSA, which is based on your NI contribution record, and income-based JSA, which is means-tested.

To qualify for JSA you must be:

- under State Pension age (although if you are aged 60–64 you can claim Pension Credit instead of income-based JSA);
- unemployed or working for less than 16 hours a week;
- capable of and available for work; and
- actively seeking work. You must have entered into a Jobseeker's Agreement, and you must comply with any directions given.

Contribution-based JSA can be paid for a maximum of 26 weeks. The rate for people aged 25 or over is £55.65. There are no additions for dependants. Although in general income and savings are not taken into account, if you have an occupational or personal pension

133

of over £50 a week this will reduce any contribution-based JSA by the amount by which your pension exceeds £50.

Income-based JSA can be paid in addition to the contribution-based JSA or on its own if you do not have sufficient NI contributions or you have already received contribution-based JSA for 26 weeks. To qualify for income-based JSA you must have no more than £8,000 savings (£12,000 if you are aged 60 or over) and a low income. If you have a partner, his or her income and savings will be added to yours and your partner must either not be in work or be working for less than 24 hours a week on average. Couples may be required to make a joint claim and both partners may need to be actively seeking work and have entered into a Jobseeker's Agreement. If your partner is over 60 or cannot work, for example because they are disabled or a carer, or if they are working at least 16 hours a week but less than 24, they will not have to meet the jobseeking requirements.

If you qualify for income-based JSA you may also get other benefits such as Housing Benefit and Council Tax Benefit and help with NHS costs. If you are under State Pension age and do not have to sign on in order to receive benefit (for example because you are a carer receiving Carer's Allowance), then you can claim Income Support instead of income-based JSA. If you are aged 60 or over, you can claim Pension Credit.

How to claim

You claim JSA from your local Jobcentre Plus office, where you will be given a claim pack and an interview will be arranged. You will need to complete a claim form which covers information needed to check your entitlement to benefit and details of the type of work you are looking for. At your interview an adviser should discuss benefits and other support, as well as covering employment options. At the end of the interview you will have to sign a Jobseeker's Agreement which outlines the action you are expected to take to find work. Once JSA is awarded, you will need to attend your local office every two weeks.

In some situations benefit may be stopped for a limited period. For example, if you leave work voluntarily without 'just cause' or refuse a job without 'good cause', then you may lose benefit for up to 26 weeks. You may lose benefit if you accept early retirement, although not if you are made redundant.

If you are refused benefit or need more information or help or advice with claiming JSA, contact a local advice agency.

Schemes to help people back to work

The Government's 'New Deal' programme aims to help people into work. It includes the New Deal for Disabled People and the New Deal for Long-Term Unemployed. There is also a 'New Deal for over 50's'. Under the scheme people are offered assistance from a personal adviser, job search support and an in-work training subsidy. You should also get financial help from the 50 plus element of Working Tax Credit.

There are also other specific measures to encourage people to work, including the 'Back to work bonus' and the continuation of Housing Benefit and Council Tax Benefit for an extra four weeks after you start work and your JSA stops.

Contact your local Jobcentre Plus office for more information.

INCOME SUPPORT

Income Support is a means-tested benefit which is intended to help with basic weekly living costs. The information here applies to people under 60 – when you reach 60 you may be able to get Pension

Credit instead (see pages 40–63). Income Support is paid to people who do not have to sign on for work; for example people who can't work because they are carers or people who are sick or disabled.

Income Support can be paid on its own if you have no other income, or it can top up other benefits or part-time earnings. If you don't have much money coming in and have no more than £8,000 in savings, it is worth checking to see if you can qualify for Income Support. You cannot get Income Support if you work 16 hours a week or more or if your partner works 24 hours a week or more.

The amount of Income Support paid will vary according to your age, existing income and savings, and entitlement to any premiums. Premiums are awarded to people receiving certain disability benefits, carers and people with dependent children, for example. Homeowners may get some help with certain housing costs. When working out your benefit some income (such as Disability Living Allowance) is not taken into account.

To claim Income Support, contact your local Jobcentre Plus office. If you need more advice about Income Support, contact a local advice agency.

BEREAVEMENT BENEFITS

This section covers the bereavement benefits that men and women widowed before State Pension age may be entitled to. It does not cover the position for people with dependent children who should seek further information from a local advice agency.

People widowed on or after 9 April 2001 may be entitled to the Bereavement Payment and the Bereavement Allowance. These apply to both men and women and are based on their late spouse's contribution record. Before April 2001 benefits were only given to widows. When you register the death the Registrar will give you a form to send to the social security office in order to claim these benefits.

Women widowed before 9 April 2001 may be receiving Widow's Pension. People widowed after State Pension age may be entitled to claim a State Pension based on their late husband's or wife's contributions, as explained on pages 6–8.

Bereavement Payment

The Bereavement Payment is a single lump-sum payment of £2,000. It is tax free and is paid mainly to widows and widowers under State Pension age. If you are over State Pension age when your spouse dies, you will still receive the payment provided that your spouse was under State Pension age or was over State Pension age (currently 60 for women, 65 for men) but not receiving a State Retirement Pension based on his or her own contribution record.

The Bereavement Payment replaced the Widow's Payment which was a £1,000 payment made only to widows (mainly those under the age of 60) before April 2001.

Bereavement Allowance

The Bereavement Allowance is paid to both men and women who are aged at least 45 but under State Pension age when they are widowed and whose spouse fulfilled the contribution conditions. The full rate is £79.60 but you will get less if you were widowed before the age of 55. You cannot receive any of your spouse's Additional State Pension. Bereavement Allowance will be paid for a maximum of 52 weeks but will stop sooner if you remarry or reach State Pension age during that period. Once you reach State Pension age you may be able to claim a State Pension based on your late husband's or wife's contributions, as explained on pages 6–8.

If you claim Income Support or Jobseeker's Allowance, when the Bereavement Allowance ends you may receive an extra £23.95 through the bereavement premium (provided that you were 55 or over but under 60 on 9 April 2001 and widowed before April 2006).

Widow's Pension

If your husband died before 9 April 2001, you may be in receipt of a Widow's Pension and this will not have been affected by the introduction of the new bereavement benefits. The full standard rate is £79.60 but you may be getting less if you were under 55 when you were widowed or if your husband did not have a full contribution record. You may also be receiving an Additional State Pension based on your husband's earnings since 1978, taking into account any periods that he was contracted out of SERPS.

When you reach State Pension age (60), you can draw the State Pension instead of the Widow's Pension or you can remain on the Widow's Pension until you reach 65. The amounts will often be the same, but you may also receive some Graduated Pension with the State Pension. Check with your social security office what the different amounts would be.

The Widow's Pension will not be affected by your earnings. However, if you do not draw your State Pension at the age of 60, you will not earn extra pension unless you give up the Widow's Pension.

If you remarry before you reach 60, you will lose the Widow's Pension. It will also be suspended during any period when you live with a man as his wife. However, if you are 60 or over and receive a

State Pension based on your previous husband's contributions, you will not lose this if you remarry or live with someone.

See social security guide NP45 *A Guide to Bereavement Benefits* and leaflet GL14 *Widowed?*

HOUSEHOLD BILLS, INSULATION AND REPAIRS

This section looks at some of the main household bills and expenses that older people face. It briefly covers dealing with debt and then summarises the help that may be available for different expenses, referring you to Age Concern factsheets and other sources of information where appropriate. More detailed information is given about: paying for fuel and insulation; help with repairs; and the Council Tax.

Debt problems

Many older people have to manage on low incomes and sometimes face particular problems when an unexpected bill comes in or income drops because of a change in circumstances such as divorce or bereavement. If you are having difficulty managing, check to see whether you are entitled to any additional income such as the benefits described in this book (for example Pension Credit, Housing Benefit or Council Tax Benefit). Then write down the amount of money you need for essential everyday living. This should help you to work out a statement of income and expenditure which you can then use to negotiate smaller payments to your creditors. Many people underestimate their basic living expenses and then try to pay their bills at a higher rate then they can really afford. Once they see the reality of your situation, most creditors should freeze interest and accept payments that you can afford.

If this seems too much to have to deal with, seek advice. There are many independent advice agencies which can help with debt problems, including the Citizens Advice Bureaux or you can ring National Debtline on Freephone 0808 808 4000.

See the Age Concern Books publication *Managing Debt*, details of which are on page 185. This may be available in your local library.

Help with bills and expenses

Fuel: There are no regular weekly social security payments towards fuel bills but there are Winter Fuel Payments and Cold Weather Payments, as described below. Grants towards insulation and draughtproofing may help you heat your home more effectively.

Rent and mortgage costs: Help towards rent comes through Housing Benefit (see pages 63–84), while homeowners may get help with their mortgage interest payments and certain service charges through Pension Credit (see pages 40–63).

Council Tax: Council Tax Benefit (see pages 63–84) is means-tested. There are also other ways of reducing Council Tax bills, which are described on pages 149–151.

Water rates: There are no social security benefits to help with the cost of water rates or sewerage charges. Some water companies have charitable funds to help people in financial need. In Scotland the system is different. Contact your local council or water company for details.

Telephone costs: There is no national scheme providing financial help with telephone charges. Some people who are sick or disabled may be able to receive help from their local authority social services department.

Repairs, improvements and adaptations: In some situations you may be able to receive a grant to help with household repairs or improvements, as explained on pages 146–149.

PAYING FOR FUEL AND INSULATION

The cost of fuel is a major expense for most pensioners. This section outlines what help is available.

Fuel debts

All gas and electricity suppliers must offer special services to people of pensionable age and people who are chronically sick or disabled. These services include not disconnecting supplies for non-payment of bills during the winter months to households where all the occupants are pensioners. Other services that you would be entitled to are: an annual free safety check for gas customers; provision of special controls or adaptors for meters and electrical appliances; and repositioning of a meter if it would be more convenient. Let your gas or electricity supplier know that you want to register for these services.

'Fuel direct'

If you have a fuel debt and are receiving Pension Credit or income-based Jobseeker's Allowance (JSA), you may be able to avoid disconnection or get reconnected by going on 'fuel direct'. Some of your benefit will be withheld every week and paid direct to the company. If you think that too large an amount is being withheld, ask the social security office whether the company will accept a smaller amount.

Winter Fuel Payments

Winter Fuel Payments started in Winter 1997–1998 to provide help with the cost of fuel bills for pensioner households. They are made to most people aged 60 or over living in Great Britain and there are no income or savings limits. The payments are based on someone's age and other circumstances in the week beginning with the third Monday in September.

The Winter Fuel Payment is £200 for most eligible households and from Winter 2003–2004 onwards an extra £100 is paid where someone in the household is aged 80 or over.

The rules for payments for Winter 2004–2005 are expected to be broadly similar to those in Winter 2003–2004. However, in previous years there were some differences in the way that payments were made, depending on whether or not someone was receiving Minimum Income Guarantee (MIG). Pension Credit has now replaced MIG, and at the time of writing it is not yet known whether the rules previously applied to those in receipt of MIG will apply to people receiving either part of Pension Credit or just to those who receive Pension Credit guarantee credit.

If you or your partner do not receive Pension Credit (this may apply just to Pension Credit guarantee credit or to both parts of Pension Credit – see above) or income-based Jobseeker's Allowance: If you are aged 60 or over, you should get £200 if you are the only person in the household entitled to a payment and £100 if you share a household with one or more other people entitled to a payment – for example a married couple, or two friends living together, will each receive £100. If you are 80 or over, you will get an additional £100 if you are the only person in your household aged 80 or over, or an additional £50 if there are one or more other people aged 80 or over.

If you are receiving Pension Credit (this may apply just to Pension Credit guarantee credit or to both parts of Pension Credit – see above) or income-based Jobseeker's Allowance:

You should receive £200 (or £300 if you or your partner are 80 or over) regardless of who else is in the household. If you are one of a couple and your partner receives Pension Credit, then he or she will receive £200 (or £300 if one of you is 80 or over) on behalf of both of you and you will not get a payment.

Some people are not eligible for payments – for example people living permanently in a care home who receive certain benefits, and people who have been in hospital for more than 52 weeks, will not get a payment. People living in a care home who are not excluded because of the benefits they receive will normally get £100 (or £150 if they are 80 or over).

If you are receiving a State Pension, Pension Credit or certain other benefits (excluding Housing Benefit and Council Tax Benefit), or if you received a payment last winter, then you should not need to claim as payments will normally be made automatically before Christmas. In other circumstances – for example if you are a man aged 60 not receiving any State benefits – you will need to make a claim. The Pension Service runs a Winter Fuel Payment helpline which people can contact to make a claim or if they have questions about the payments. The number is 08459 15 15 15. If you need to make a claim for the payment for Winter 2004–2005, your claim must be received by 30 March 2005. However, there is no time limit for claims for the first three winters (ie 1997–1998, 1998–1999 and 1999–2000).

Although payments are normally only made to people living in Britain, some people who qualify for a Winter Fuel Payment in Britain and move to another European Economic Area country, or Switzerland or Gibraltar, may be able to continue to receive payments. For more information on this specific issue ring 029 2042 8635.

Cold Weather Payments

If you receive Pension Credit or income-based JSA which includes a pensioner or disability premium, you may be eligible for Cold Weather Payments. A payment of £8.50 is made when the average temperature at a specified weather station has been recorded as, or is forecast to be, 0° Celsius or below over seven consecutive days. Savings are not taken into account. These payments will be made automatically, so you do not have to make a claim.

Grants for energy efficiency

If you live in England

The Warm Front Grant provides a package, up to the value of £1,500, of energy efficiency insulation and heating measures tailored to each property. It might include cavity and loft insulation, draughtproofing, hot water tank insulation, gas room heaters with thermostat controls, converting a solid-fuel open fire to modern glass-fronted fire, energy efficiency advice and low-energy light bulbs. You are eligible for this grant if you are a householder in receipt of Attendance Allowance, Disability Living Allowance or certain other disability benefits.

The Warm Front Grant Plus provides a package of energy efficiency and heating measures, including central heating, up to the value of £2,500. To qualify, you have to be a householder aged 60 or over and in receipt of Pension Credit, Housing Benefit, Council Tax Benefit or income-based Jobseeker's Allowance.

For more information about the grant, contact EAGA Partnership on Freephone 0800 316 2808.

If you live in Wales

The Home Energy Efficiency Scheme in Wales provides grants for people aged 60 or over who are receiving one of the following income-related benefits: Pension Credit, Housing Benefit, Council Tax Benefit, income-based Jobseeker's Allowance or certain disability benefits including Disability Living Allowance or Attendance Allowance. The grant will offer a variety of insulation measures, including cavity wall and loft insulation and the installation of gas or electric central heating. The maximum grant is £1,500 (or £2,700 including gas central heating or storage heating where there is no gas supply).

For more information about the grants, contact EAGA on Freephone 0800 316 2815.

See Age Concern Factsheet 1 *Help with Heating*.

If you live in Scotland

In Scotland energy grants are made under the Warm Deal scheme. The grant covers a package of energy efficiency measures, all or some of which may be offered, according to the energy needs of the home. Grants may be offered to homeowners and tenants (including council tenants) who receive any or more of the following income-related benefits: Pension Credit, Housing Benefit, Council Tax Benefit, income-based Jobseeker's Allowance or certain disability benefits including Disability Living Allowance or Attendance Allowance.

The maximum grant is £500 and may cover the following energy efficiency measures: cavity wall insulation; loft insulation; draughtproofing; hot and cold tank and pipe insulation; energy advice; and up to four energy efficient light bulbs. The scheme is administered by EAGA Partnership which can arrange for a registered installer to do the work. If you want to carry out the work yourself, a lower grant of up to £40 is available to cover the cost of materials, but you must not buy any materials until authorised by EAGA. Those over 60, but not in receipt of any of the benefits listed above, may qualify for a reduced grant of £125 or 25 per cent of the cost of the work, whichever is the lower.

For more information about the grants, contact EAGA on Freephone 0800 072 0150.

The Scottish Executive is working to provide free central heating for every pensioner and for all those in local authority housing in Scotland who do not currently have central heating. (From 1 April 2004, the Central Heating Programme has been extended to people who are aged 80 and over and who have partial or inefficient central heating.) Work will continue on this project until 2006. Free central heating is available regardless of income or savings, and the scheme covers up to £2,500 worth of work. EAGA Partnership administers the scheme for privately rented and owner occupied housing. You can contact EAGA on 0800 316 1653 for more details. If you live in council or housing association accommodation, your landlord will be able to give you more details about work they will do under the scheme.

See Age Concern Factsheet 1s *Help with Heating* (the Scottish version).

HELP WITH REPAIRS, IMPROVEMENTS AND ADAPTATIONS

England and Wales

The Government has made changes to the grants system for helping homeowners to pay for repairs and home improvements. Under the new reforms local authorities no longer have to give home improvement grants or home repair assistance, but have the powers to provide assistance for repairs, improvements and adaptations to housing.

The assistance provided by the local authority may be provided in any form, including loans, grants, labour, materials or advice. It might be provided unconditionally, or subject to conditions such as repayment of all or part of the assistance or a contribution towards the work for which assistance is required. The local authority has to have a published policy setting out the type of assistance it will provide and in what circumstances. It should also tell you how to make an enquiry and apply for assistance. A summary of the policy must be available to the public on request.

Local authorities must still provide mandatory disabled facilities grants. A disabled facilities grant is mandatory in specific circumstances. It must be given if you are disabled and do not have access to your home and to the basic amenities within it (such as a bathroom, toilet or kitchen), provided that you qualify on income grounds – the grants are means tested. If you receive Pension Credit you will not normally have to make a contribution. The system is complicated and you might find it useful to get further information from the local authority or other agency such as a local Age Concern. A step-by-step guide on how to work out your contribution is included in *The Disability Rights Handbook* (see page 181).

The formal application for the grant must be made to the housing department of the local authority (council). The housing department must consult with the social services department to decide if the adaptations are necessary and appropriate. This will normally mean that you will receive a visit from an occupational therapist from social services to assess your needs and make recommendations on what work needs to be done.

The maximum amount for a mandatory disabled facilities grant is £25,000 in England and £30,000 in Wales.

Discretionary disabled facilities grants have been abolished but local authorities are able to give discretionary assistance for adaptations or to help the occupant to move to alternative accommodation. There is no restriction on the amount of assistance that may be given. It may be paid in addition, or as an alternative to, the grant.

You should not start the work or buy any of the materials until you have received the local authority's approval to go ahead.

If you receive Pension Credit you may be able to claim a discretionary Community Care Grant or Budgeting Loan for minor household repairs (see pages 84–88).

In some areas there are Home Improvement Agencies (sometimes called Care and Repair or Staying Put projects) which give advice and practical assistance to vulnerable homeowners, such as older people or disabled people, on getting repairs, improvements or adaptation work carried out. Your local authority or local Age Concern should know whether there is a scheme in your area or contact *foundations*, the national co-ordinating body for Home Improvement Agencies, at the address on page 178.

See Age Concern Factsheet 13 *Older Homeowners: Financial Help with Repairs and Adaptations*.

Scotland

In Scotland the system of grants is different and only brief information is given here. Grants may be available from the local authority housing department to owners and private tenants to help meet the cost of improvement and repair work. Most grants are discretionary but you must be awarded a grant in some circumstances; for example if your home lacks certain standard amenities. You may also get help towards the costs of housing aids and adaptations if you are assessed by the social work department as needing these. In some areas there are Care and Repair schemes (see above).

For details of grants, or to find out if there is a Care and Repair scheme in your area, contact your local authority housing department or see Age Concern Factsheet 13s *Older Homeowners: Financial Help With Repairs and Adaptations* (the Scottish version).

HELP WITH THE COUNCIL TAX

The Council Tax is the system of paying towards local government services in England, Scotland and Wales. The rates system continues in Northern Ireland. Under the Council Tax system all domestic dwellings are allocated to one of eight bands (A–H) depending on their estimated value in April 1991. The level of tax for a property in band H will be three times as high as the tax for a property in band A. One bill will be sent to each household. One or more people will be legally responsible for paying the bill, although the household can choose how to divide up the bill.

The banding system in Wales will be changed in April 2005 to nine bands (A–I) based on property values in April 2003. In England it is planned that the banding system will be changed from April 2007, based on property values at April 2005.

Extra £100 for people aged 70 and over

In the March 2004 Budget, the Chancellor announced that this year there will be an extra £100 paid to households with someone aged 70 or over in recognition of the difficulties that many older pensioners face in meeting Council Tax bills. This will be in addition to the Winter Fuel Payment and any other entitlements. At the time of writing no further information is available about how or when these payments will be made.

Reducing your bill

There are various ways that your bill may be reduced and these are summarised below. It may be possible to receive help from more than one of these schemes.

Exemptions Some properties, mainly certain empty ones, will be exempt, which means that there will be no Council Tax to pay. For example, your former home will be exempt if it is empty because you are living in a hospital or care home, or because you have gone to live with someone else in order to receive or provide personal care. A property is also exempt if a severely mentally impaired person lives there alone and would be liable to pay the tax.

Disability reduction scheme The property may be placed in a lower band if it has certain features which are important for a disabled person, such as extra space for a wheelchair or an additional bathroom or kitchen for the use of the disabled person. If your home qualifies for a reduction, your bill will be reduced to the level of tax for the band below the one your home is in. Since April 2000 properties in the lowest band (A) that have the relevant disability features have also qualified for a reduction. In this situation bills will be reduced by one sixth. Contact your local authority if you think that your property would qualify for a reduction.

Discounts The Council Tax assumes that there are two or more people living in each property. A discount of a quarter (25 per cent) will be given if someone lives alone and a discount of half (50 per cent) will normally be given if no one is living there. However, some people will not be counted for the purposes of the Council Tax, so discounts may still be given even if there are two or more people in a property. For example, someone who is 'severely mentally impaired' will not be counted. The discount can also apply to a carer who lives with and, for at least 35 hours a week, is caring for someone receiving the highest care component of Disability Living Allowance or the higher rate of Attendance Allowance. You will not get this discount, however, if the person you care for is your partner or is a child under 18.

Council Tax Benefit This depends on the income and savings of the person(s) responsible for the bill or the people they live with. It is described in more detail on pages 63–84.

See Age Concern Factsheet 21 *The Council Tax*.

HELP WITH HEALTH COSTS

Most of the treatment given under the National Health Service (NHS) is free, but there are some things for which most people have to pay part or all of the cost. This section first outlines hearing and chiropody services. It then explains who can get help with the cost of other NHS services such as dental care, eye tests and glasses.

Free NHS services

Hearing aids

You should discuss hearing difficulties with your GP who may, if necessary, refer you to a hospital for tests. If you are prescribed a hearing aid, this will be fitted and issued by a local NHS hearing aid centre. NHS hearing aids are available on free loan; replacements and batteries are also free. It is possible to buy private hearing aids, but these can be expensive and are not necessarily more effective.

The Royal National Institute for Deaf People (RNID) produces a range of information leaflets on hearing loss, hearing aids (including digital hearing aids) and other matters concerning deafness – see address on page 179. The RNID can also tell you about the NHS Modernising

Hearing Aid Services programme, which aims to improve patient services as well as making the latest digital hearing aid technology available through all hearing aid centres by April 2005 (2007 in Scotland).

Chiropody/podiatry

NHS chiropody/podiatry services are free to those with a clinical need but there is some variation in the extent of the provision. In many areas, there will be eligibility criteria which you must meet in order to be treated as an NHS patient. Your GP or Primary Care Trust should be able to advise you about local NHS chiropody/podiatry services.

Some services are liaising with voluntary organisations, such as Age Concern, or with family members, to provide nail cutting services, and providing education in foot care to prevent problems. The Age Concern Information Line on Freephone 0800 00 99 66 will be able to give you the contact details for your nearest Age Concern. Contact Age Concern locally to see if it offers this service and whether there is a charge.

If you wish to consider private treatment, your local NHS health care provider may have details. Alternatively you may wish to refer to *Yellow Pages* or look at the website of the Society of Chiropodists and Podiatrists (www.feetforlife.org). Make sure that the chiropodist is registered with the Health Professions Council.

Help with NHS costs

If you (or your partner if you have one) receive Pension Credit guarantee credit, Income Support or income-based Jobseeker's Allowance (JSA), you are entitled to receive help with the health costs described below by showing your order book or award notice or a letter from the social security office. If you receive Working Tax Credit with Child Tax Credit or with a disability element (check your award notice), you may also get this help, depending on the level of your income. In the following paragraphs, wherever Pension Credit guarantee credit or Income Support are mentioned it also covers these other benefits. In certain circumstances help may also be available to people receiving a War Pension.

If you are not in receipt of one of the benefits mentioned above but have no more than £12,000 (£8,000 if you are aged under 60) in savings, you can apply for help with costs of NHS dental treatment, glasses or contact lenses, and hospital travel costs through the NHS Low Income Scheme. (The limit for people living permanently in care homes is different – £20,000 in England, Scotland and Wales.)

If you qualify for help with health costs you will be sent one of two certificates. Certificate HC2 entitles you to full help with health costs including free prescriptions, dental treatment, glasses or hospital travel costs. If your income is higher, you may get certificate HC3, which entitles you to partial help with health costs and you are not entitled to help with prescription charges. The certificate normally lasts for 12 months.

To apply for a certificate you will need to complete the form HC1. This is available from your local social security office or NHS hospital; some dentists, opticians and GP surgeries also have them. (If you live permanently in a care home and receive financial support from the local authority, ask the owner of the home for form HC1 (SC).) It is best to apply in advance. Remember that if you receive Pension Credit guarantee credit, you do not need to apply for a certificate.

See Department of Health leaflet HC11 *Help with Health Costs* or the Age Concern Information Sheet IS20 *Help with Health Costs for Older People.*

Prescriptions

NHS prescriptions are free to people aged 60 or over. However, younger adults can also get free prescriptions if they have a low income or suffer from a 'specified medical condition' (these are listed in leaflet HC11) and hold an exemption certificate.

Prescriptions are free to partners aged under 60 of people receiving Pension Credit guarantee credit and those who have a valid certificate HC2 on grounds of low income, as described above. People who have a valid certificate HC3 entitling them to partial help with some NHS costs cannot get free prescriptions.

If you cannot get free prescriptions but require regular prescriptions, you may be able to save money by buying a prescription prepayment certificate (PPC) for either 4 or 12 months. For information about the PPC scheme or to request an application form (FP95), you can ring 0845 850 00 30. The form is also available from pharmacists. Your pharmacist will be able to help you decide whether a PPC would be financially advantageous for you.

Dental care

NHS dental treatment, check-ups and dentures are free if you or your partner gets Pension Credit guarantee credit or if you have certificate HC2. The cost may be reduced if you have certificate HC3. Details of how to apply for a certificate are given above. Every time you start a new course of treatment, tell the dentist that you are on Pension Credit guarantee credit or have certificate HC2 or HC3. In Wales dental checks are free for all people aged 60 and over.

Unless you are entitled to free treatment or help with the costs, you will have to pay 80 per cent of the cost of most treatment up to a maximum level of £378 in England and Scotland (for courses of treatment starting on or after 1 April 2004), and £354 in Wales, for one course of treatment.

It is a good idea to make sure that you are registered with an NHS dentist for regular treatment (called 'continuing care'), as this means that you will be entitled under the NHS to any treatment that the dentist considers necessary to secure and maintain your oral health. Contact NHS Direct on 0845 46 47 for advice on how to find an NHS dentist.

● **No help is given towards private dental fees. If you want NHS dental care, make sure that the dentist is providing you with NHS treatment before you start each course. You can do this when you discuss the proposed treatment with your dentist.**

See Age Concern Factsheet 5 *Dental Care and Older People*.

Sight tests and glasses

NHS sight tests are available free to all people aged 60 or over. There is no definition of what an NHS sight test should include. Tests for conditions such as glaucoma and other eye diseases that are more likely in older people are particularly important, so always ask what tests will be included in your NHS sight test.

For more information on eye problems and NHS sight tests, contact the Royal National Institute of the Blind at the address on page 179.

Partners of people receiving Pension Credit guarantee credit who are under the age of 60 will be entitled to a free NHS sight test. Younger people will also qualify for a free NHS sight test if they or their partner have certificate HC2, as described above. Free tests are also available to people who belong to a priority group, which includes registered blind and partially sighted people, those who need complex lenses, and diagnosed diabetics. People who have glaucoma or are considered to be at risk of glaucoma, or someone aged 40 or over who is the parent, brother, sister or son or daughter of a person with diagnosed glaucoma will also qualify.

If you cannot get to the optician's practice for a sight test, you may be able to arrange for an optician to visit you at home. If you are entitled to a free NHS sight test, you will not have to pay for the visit.

You are entitled to a voucher towards the cost of glasses provided you or your partner gets Pension Credit guarantee credit or have certificate HC2. You may get some help if you have certificate HC3. You may be able to claim a refund in some circumstances if you do not receive your certificate in time, but it is better to apply well in advance. The voucher carries a financial value linked to your optical prescription; it may cover the full cost of the glasses or be used as part payment for a more expensive pair. If your glasses or contact lenses cost more than any voucher you are given, you will have to pay the difference. If you need complex lenses, you will be able to receive a voucher from your optician to help pay for the glasses regardless of income and savings. However, the amount of help will be greater if you or your partner receives Pension Credit guarantee credit or qualifies on grounds of low income.

You do not have to get your glasses from the optician who does your sight test, although you may choose to do so. If you prefer to obtain your glasses from a different optician, simply take your prescription (and any voucher to which you are entitled) with you.

Before you have a sight test or get glasses, find out whether you qualify for help. If you will have to pay for some or all of the cost, it is best to 'shop around' to check whether another optician might be cheaper, as charges can vary.

People with serious eye conditions and who require specialist hospital care only have to pay up to a maximum charge and the hospital then meets the difference between the maximum charge and the cost of the glasses.

Elastic hosiery, wigs, fabric supports

Elastic support stockings are available on prescription, and are free to both men and women aged 60 or over. Support tights are available only through the hospital service but will be free to people who are entitled to free prescriptions; for example if they receive Pension Credit guarantee credit or have certificate HC2.

Wigs and fabric supports are supplied through hospitals and are free for inpatients. If you are an outpatient, there are charges depending on the type of wig or fabric support supplied. However, they are free if you are on Pension Credit guarantee credit or have certificate HC2; if you have certificate HC3, you may get some help with the cost.

Hospital travel costs

If you get Pension Credit guarantee credit, you are entitled to help with the necessary costs of travelling to and from hospital (or other place) for NHS treatment under the care of a consultant. If you have certificate HC2 or HC3 on grounds of low income, you may get help towards these costs. See 'Help with NHS costs' above on how to apply for a certificate. If you are not sure what help you can get, contact the hospital before you travel. Hospitals will not normally reimburse taxi fares unless taxis are the only transport available – check with the hospital first.

If you qualify for help with travel costs and it is medically necessary for you to have a companion to accompany you, their travel costs should also be covered. However, they can only be claimed when they are certified to be necessary in the opinion of a doctor or appropriate health professional – so check with the hospital before you travel to ensure that you have the necessary permission or written confirmation.

If you are visiting a close relative in hospital and you are receiving Pension Credit guarantee credit, you may be able to get help with the cost of your fares from the Social Fund (see pages 84–88).

Health care outside the UK

As a UK resident, you are covered by the NHS only while you are in the UK. If you are abroad on business or on holiday and fall ill, you may have to pay all or part of the cost of any treatment. There are special arrangements with member states of the European Economic Area (EEA) plus Switzerland (see page vii), and some other countries which may enable you to get free or reduced cost *emergency* medical care during a visit abroad.

Before going abroad, get the leaflet *Health Advice for Travellers* from the local post office or by telephoning the Health Literature line (Freephone 0800 555 777). This leaflet will tell you what cover there might be for UK residents in the EEA (including Switzerland) and some other countries with which the UK has a reciprocal agreement for emergency treatment. It also includes an application for a Form E111. This form applies to travel in the EEA and Switzerland only.

If you are travelling to an EEA country for a holiday or short business trip and do not already have a stamped Form E111, complete the application form for the Form E111 and the E111 itself and take them to a post office where the E111 will be validated. The E111 is then valid indefinitely as long as there are no changes which affect the details on the Form and you remain at the same address. Take the E111 and a photocopy of it with you as both may be required in some countries if you need to use it.

Depending on what country you are going to, Form E111 will entitle you to the same medical treatment *in an emergency* as residents of the EEA country you are visiting. The Form is *not* a substitute for holiday insurance and will only provide you with basic medical care in the event of an emergency. Not all doctors practising in an EEA country will be working within the state health system. Therefore if you do have to visit a doctor in the community for emergency treatment, as opposed to a hospital emergency department, you will need to check whether your E111 is acceptable to secure treatment and any medication necessary free of charge or at a reduced cost.

It is advisable to take out private medical insurance to cover the full cost of any treatment you may need abroad whether you are going to an EEA or non-EEA country. Medical treatment is very expensive, as is the cost of bringing a person back to the UK in the event of illness or death.

The *Health Advice for Travellers* leaflet also contains general guidance on immunisation requirements for travellers. You are entitled to typhoid, polio and hepatitis A vaccines on the NHS: their administration is free and prescription charges follow the patient's normal entitlement (free for people aged 60 and over, for example). All other travel immunisations are non-NHS and are likely to incur a variable charge.

If you are going to live permanently or for a large part of the year in another country, you should find out well in advance about your entitlement to medical treatment there. If you plan to return to the UK for holidays or for longer periods of time, you should also check your entitlement to treatment while you are back in the UK. Legislation came into force on 1 April 2004 that allows UK pensioners to reside in the UK for at least six months and in another EEA country for less than six months each year and still be eligible for free NHS treatment.

TRAVEL AND OTHER CONCESSIONS

TRAVEL

Rail and underground

All rail companies give one-third reductions on most types of ticket to people who have a Senior Railcard, which currently costs £18 (March

2004) and is valid for one year. It is available to people aged 60 or over, provided proof of age is given. Leaflets with application forms should be available from principal railway stations.

If you are disabled, you can buy a Disabled Person's Railcard, which currently costs £14, and which allows you and a companion to travel at a third off most standard fares. Full details of who qualifies are given in a leaflet available from many railway stations.

Underground or other transport systems may also offer concessions; you should ask at local offices.

Bus services

In England, there is a national minimum bus concession scheme. While some local authorities may offer better concessions, all authorities must offer a minimum concession of half fare, for travel after 9.30 am, for all people aged 60 or over. Travel is limited to within the issuing local authority but some local neighbouring authorities have joint arrangements.

In Scotland, people aged 60 and over are entitled to free off-peak local bus travel, restricted to within each local authority area. Some (but not all) local authorities, however, have joined together to enable arrangements which allow free bus travel across local authority boundaries.

In Wales, people aged 60 and over are entitled to free bus passes and free local bus travel within their own local authority.

Apply to your local authority (London or metropolitan borough, district council or unitary authority) for details.

Coach services

National Express offers up to 30 per cent off many standard fares for holders of the Advantage50 Discount Coachcard. This card is available to anyone aged 50 and over and costs £10 a year (March 2004). A three-year card that costs £19 is also available. The discounts are offered on all National Express coach services within England and Wales, and on some services to Scotland. Details of these concessions are obtainable from any appointed National Express agent. Other coach operators will also give concessions, but may have different age limits.

Since 1 May 2003 people who are 60 and over, and people who have a local authority concessionary travel pass because they are disabled, have been able to get coach fares at half price in England and Wales. Participation in this scheme is voluntary but National Express, the major provider, is a part of the scheme. The offer might not be available during some peak periods or on Apex tickets.

In Scotland the same rules apply as for bus concessions, with free off-peak travel within the local authority or travel scheme area.

Taxicard schemes

Some local authorities operate Taxicard schemes which provide reduced fares for disabled people. Contact your local authority to find out if it runs a scheme.

Airlines

Some airlines may have concessionary fares for pensioners. Ask at the airline or travel agent for details.

See Age Concern Factsheet 26 *Travel Information for Older People*.

OTHER CONCESSIONS

People over a certain age or who are entitled to a State Pension may be able to receive concessions such as: reductions at leisure centres and swimming pools; lower admission prices to museums or other places of interest; or reduced fees for joining adult education classes. Most national museums are free for people aged 60 or over. Sometimes local businesses such as hairdressers may have special rates at certain times of the week. These concessions vary, so look out for any reductions that might apply to you.

Television licences

Television licences are free for households with a person aged 75 and over. For more information, contact the TV licensing information helpline on 0870 241 6468.

There are two other types of concession. People who are registered blind can obtain a 50 per cent reduction from the full licence fee. It is also possible to get specially adapted TV sound receivers and these do not need a licence to operate. Some people over the age of 60 who live in care homes or certain local authority or housing association sheltered accommodation qualify for a concessionary £5 licence.

See Age Concern England Factsheet 3 *Television Licence Concessions*.

Proof of eligibility

If you are drawing a pension but do not have a pension book (for example because your pension is paid into an account by Direct Payment), you can get a card proving that you are a pensioner. Write, quoting your pension number, to The Pension Service, Tyneview Park,

Whitley Road, Benton, Newcastle upon Tyne NE98 1BA. If you have no proof of being a pensioner, you may have to produce a copy of your birth certificate or another official document showing your age.

HELP FROM CHARITIES OR BENEVOLENT FUNDS

If you have checked that you are getting all the benefits you are entitled to and it is still hard to manage financially, you could try asking for help from charities or benevolent funds. Assistance may be available either as a lump sum or regular weekly payments. If you are receiving Pension Credit (see pages 40–63), all charitable payments made to you will be ignored.

Benevolent funds help people in particular circumstances. For example these might be based on your occupation (or former occupation) or that of your partner; any health problems or disabilities you may have; or the area where you live. Others may help people who are members of trade unions or who have a particular religious belief.

To find out more information you could contact a local advice agency. There are also two national organisations – The Association of Charity Officers (incorporating the Occupational Benevolent Funds Alliance) and Charity Search – that can help put people in contact with charities and benevolent funds. Their addresses are on pages 176 and 177.

LEGAL FEES, WILLS AND FUNERALS

Help with legal costs and making wills

If you need help with a legal problem, you may be able to obtain this free from a local advice agency or you may be able to get help with

163

the cost of a solicitor's fees through the Community Legal Service run by the Legal Services Commission.

If you are on Pension Credit, Income Support or income-based Jobseeker's Allowance or have a low income and little or no savings, you may be able to obtain help with legal advice and representation through the different schemes. This can include help with making a will, but in England and Wales you must be 70 or over or mentally or physically disabled in order to receive help.

For further information see Age Concern Factsheet 43 *Obtaining and Paying for Legal Advice* and Factsheet 7 *Making Your Will*. See also *The Community Legal Service*, available from the Legal Services Commission, St Ives Direct, Enterprise Way, Edenbridge, Kent TN8 6HF. Tel: 0845 3000 343. Website: www.legalservices.gov.uk The Scottish Legal Aid Board also publishes helpful leaflets on Legal Aid. Its address is 44 Drumsheugh Gardens, Edinburgh EH3 7SW. Tel: 0131 226 7061. Website: www.slab.org.uk

---

Help with Funeral Payments

This section describes the Funeral Payments available from the Social Fund which are part of the social security system. For more details about arranging a funeral, including information about the duty of local and health authorities to pay for certain funerals, see Age Concern Factsheet 27 *Planning for a Funeral*.

You may be able to receive a Social Fund Funeral Payment towards the cost of a funeral if you have good reason for taking responsibility for the expenses and you or your partner is receiving Pension Credit, Income Support, Housing Benefit, Council Tax Benefit, income-based Jobseeker's Allowance or Working Tax Credit where a disabled person is included in the assessment. Any savings you have will not be taken into account. However, as explained below, there are restrictions on who can receive a payment and limits on the amount of the payment, so it is important to check what you are entitled to before making the arrangements.

To receive a payment you should be the partner of the person who has died, or someone else who it is reasonable to expect to take responsibility for arranging the funeral. The person who died must have been resident in the UK and the funeral must normally take place in the UK but in some circumstances it can take place elsewhere in the European Economic Area.

Unless you are the partner of the person who has died, the social security decision maker may decide, based on the nature and extent of your contact with the person who has died, that it was not reasonable for you to have taken responsibility for the funeral costs. There may, for example, be another close relative who is not receiving a qualifying benefit.

The payment can cover necessary burial and cremation costs, certain necessary travel expenses and up to £700 for other funeral expenses.

Although your savings do not affect your entitlement to a Funeral Payment, if there is money available from the estate of the person who has died, or money from insurance policies or pre-paid funeral plans, this will be deducted from any award that would have been made.

To make a claim you will need form SF200 from your social security office. You have to claim within three months of the funeral, but it is advisable to check what you are entitled to before arranging a funeral.

See social security leaflet D49 *What To Do After a Death* and Age Concern Factsheet 27 *Planning for a Funeral*.

FURTHER INFORMATION

This part of *Your Rights* gives details about local and national sources of help to contact for assistance and advice. In addition, there is information about obtaining Department for Work and Pensions (DWP) social security leaflets, Age Concern factsheets, and other publications on social security benefits mentioned in the book. Also included is an index to help you find the information you require in this book and a summary of the main benefit rates.

| DEPARTMENT FOR WORK AND PENSIONS |

Much of the information in *Your Rights* covers State Pensions and social security benefits. The government department responsible is the Department for Work and Pensions (DWP). It replaced the Department of Social Security (DSS) in 2001. The rules for State Pensions and social security benefits and the levels of payment are set out in legislation – for example, each year regulations are agreed in Parliament setting out the annual increases to pensions and benefits.

In April 2002, The Pension Service, Jobcentre Plus and the Disability and Carers Service replaced the Benefits Agency and Employment Service. The Pension Service is responsible for State Pensions, Pension Credit and Winer Fuel Payments, and for providing information about other pension-related entitlements, including State Pension forecasts to help those of working age in planning for their future.

Jobcentre Plus deals with people of working age by administering social security benefits and providing advice and support about employment opportunities.

The Disability and Carers Service is responsible for Attendance Allowance, Disability Living Allowance and Carer's Allowance.

The Pension Service delivers services and products through a network of pension centres across England, Scotland and Wales. The pension centres deal with customers by telephone, post or email, and are supported by a local service which offers face to face contact.

To contact The Pension Service telephone 0845 606 0265 (textphone: 0845 606 0285) – this will connect you with the pension centre covering your area. Staff there will provide information and answer queries about your State Pension and other pension-related entitlements. They can also tell you about local service, including

167

details of surgeries held in your area and home visits. You can find the postal or email address of your pension centre at www.thepensionservice.gov.uk/contact If your State Pension is paid direct into an account, you should continue to deal with Pensions Direct on 0845 301 3011 (textphone: 0845 301 3012).

Problems with administration

If you have a problem with the administration of a benefit – for example if there is a delay in processing your claim – you can make your complaint to The Pension Service by phone, letter or email, or by using leaflet GL22 *Tell Us Your Comments and Complaints*. If you are still dissatisfied, get in touch with a local advice agency or your MP.

National DWP addresses

The Pension Service

Tyneview Park
Whitley Road
Benton
Newcastle upon Tyne
NE98 1BA

State Pension Forecasting Service

For a State Pension forecast, telephone 0845 300 0168 (textphone: 0845 300 0169).

State Pension Teleclaims Service

To claim a State Pension, telephone 0845 300 1084 (textphone: 0845 300 2086).

Pensions Direct

Deals with changes of circumstances and enquiries for the majority of people who have their pension paid direct into an account. Telephone 0845 301 3011, 8.00am–8.00pm weekdays. Textphone: 0845 301 3012.

International Pension Centre

For information about pensions and medical cover for those who live, or have previously lived, overseas, telephone 0191 218 7777, 8.00am–8.00pm weekdays. Textphone: 0191 218 7280.

Pension Credit

To apply for Pension Credit by telephone, or to get an application form from the application line, telephone 0800 99 1234 (a free call), 8.00am–8.00pm weekdays, 9.00am–1.00pm Saturdays. Textphone: 0800 169 0133. To write for an application form, write to Freepost NAT 3780, PO Box 457, Mexborough, S64 9ZZ.

Jobcentre Plus

Details of your local 'Jobcentre Plus' office can be found in the phone book.

DWP/Pension Service websites

If you have access to the Internet, you can obtain leaflets, publications and other information from the websites. You can also download claim forms for many benefits.

Websites: www.dwp.gov.uk and www.thepensionservice.gov.uk

Disability and carers addresses

Disability and Carers Service

Warbreck House
Warbreck Hill Road
Blackpool FY2 0YE
Tel: 0845 7123456, 7.30am–6.30pm weekdays
Textphone: 0845 7224433

The Disability and Carers Service administers Disability Living Allowance and Attendance Allowance, although initial claims are normally dealt with at the regionally based Disability Benefit Centres.

Carer's Allowance Unit

Palatine House
Lancaster Road
Preston
Lancashire PR1 1HB
Tel: 01253 856123

Benefit Enquiry Line for people with disabilities

For advice and information about disability benefits, telephone 0800 88 22 00 (a free call), 8.30am–6.30pm weekdays, 9.00am–1.00pm Saturdays. Textphone: 0800 24 33 55.

Staff can arrange for help with completing forms over the phone for benefits such as Attendance Allowance and Disability Living Allowance.

AGE CONCERN INFORMATION LINE

Age Concern Information Line provides a service to older people and their relatives and friends and to carers and professionals. Contact the Line (Freephone 0800 00 99 66) to obtain the factsheets listed below (up to five are available free). The factsheets include details of the telephone number to contact if you need further information. People who live in Scotland will be sent factsheets that cover Scottish law and practice where this is different.

Community care

Consumer

Health

Housing

Income and benefits

Leisure, learning and work

For up to five free factsheets telephone 0800 00 99 66 (7am–7pm, seven days a week, every day of the year). Alternatively you may prefer to write to:

Age Concern
FREEPOST (SWB 30375)
Ashburton
Devon TQ13 7ZZ

For professionals working with older people, the factsheets are available on an annual subscription service, which includes updates throughout the year. For further details and costs of the subscription, please write to Age Concern at the above Freepost address.

LOCAL SOURCES OF HELP

Age Concern

Most areas have a local Age Concern which provides services and advice. You can find the address from the phone book, library or Citizens Advice Bureau, or you can write to the appropriate national Age Concern (addresses on page 183) or telephone the Age Concern Information Line (0800 00 99 66) for the address of the nearest local Age Concern to you.

Citizens Advice Bureau (CAB)

The local offices provide advice and information on all kinds of subjects, including social security benefits, housing and consumer problems. You can find out where your nearest CAB is from the phone book or at your local library.

Law centre

There may be a law centre giving free legal advice in your area. Check in the telephone book or at a CAB, or telephone the Community Legal Service directory line on 0845 608 1122 or look at the Law Centres Federation website at www.lawcentres.org.uk

Local authority/council

In England the structure of local government depends on whether you live in a county, or in a metropolitan or London borough, or a unitary authority. All areas in Scotland and Wales have a unitary authority. In England, if you live in a county, the district council will deal with Housing Benefit, Council Tax Benefit and other matters to do with the Council Tax. You will need to contact the county council about social services. In a metropolitan or London borough, or unitary authority, there will be just one authority that will deal with the Council

Tax, Housing Benefit and social services. Some authorities have welfare rights workers to advise on benefits. You will find the address of your local authority in the telephone book under the name of your county, unitary authority, metropolitan or London borough, or ask at your local library.

Local councillor

A councillor for your area may be able to help with problems with the local authority. You can get the names of the councillors for your 'ward' from the town hall, library or CAB.

Local Government Ombudsman

If you feel you have suffered because of maladministration in the way the local authority has dealt with your case, you can make a complaint to the Local Government Ombudsman. You can do this direct or through your local councillor. Ask a local advice agency or councillor for further information.

Member of Parliament (MP)

Your MP may be able to help with problems involving government departments. If you do not know who your MP is, ask at the town hall, library or CAB or ring the House of Commons Information Office on 020 7219 4272. Most MPs hold regular surgeries locally; or you can write to your MP at the House of Commons, London SW1A 0AA. For a complaint about unfair treatment by a government department (for example a delay with a benefit claim), ask the MP to refer your complaint to the Parliamentary Ombudsman.

In Scotland you can contact Members of the Scottish Parliament at Scottish Parliament, Edinburgh EH99 1SP. In Wales you can contact Assembly Members at the National Assembly for Wales, Cardiff Bay, Cardiff CF99 1NA (Information Line: 029 2089 8200).

Trade union

If you were a member of a trade union before retirement, it may be worth contacting your local branch, particularly for problems over a pension from work.

Welfare rights and money advice centres

There may be an independent welfare rights or money advice centre locally. Money advice centres generally deal with debt problems and may accept referrals only from other agencies.

NATIONAL SOURCES OF INFORMATION

The national organisations listed below may be able to help or put you in touch with a source of advice.

Association of Charity Officers (incorporating the Occupational Benevolent Funds Alliance)

Unicorn House
Station Close
Potters Bar
Hertfordshire EN6 3JW
Tel: 01707 651777
Website: www.aco.uk.net
Provides information about charities that make grants to individuals in need.

Carers UK

20–25 Glasshouse Yard
London EC1A 4JT
Tel: 020 7490 8818

Helpline: 0808 808 7777, weekdays 10.00am–12.00pm and
2.00pm–4.00pm
Website: www.carersonline.org.uk
Provides general advice and help for all carers.

Charity Search

25 Portview Road
Avonmouth
Bristol BS11 9LD
Tel: 0117 982 4060, Mondays–Thursdays 9.00am–3.00pm
Helps link older people with charities that may provide grants to individuals. Applications in writing are preferred.

Counsel and Care

Twyman House
16 Bonny Street
London NW1 9PG
Advice line (local rate call): 0845 300 7585, weekdays
10.00am–1.00pm
Website: www.counselandcare.org.uk
Advises on obtaining and paying for care in a care home.

Disability Alliance

Universal House
88–94 Wentworth Street
London E1 7SA
Tel: 020 7247 8776
Rights Advice Line: 020 7247 8763, Mondays and Wednesdays
2.00pm–4.00pm
Website: www.disabilityalliance.org

Produces Disability Rights Handbook *(see page 181) and other publications, and gives advice on social security benefits for disabled people through the Rights Advice Line.*

EAGA Partnership Ltd

Freepost NEA 12054
Newcastle upon Tyne NE2 1BR
Freephone: 0800 316 2808 (England)
Freephone: 0800 316 2815 (Wales)
Freephone: 0800 072 0150 (Scotland)
Website: www.eaga.co.uk
Administers the Warm Front grants in England, Home Energy Efficiency Scheme in Wales and Warm Deal and Central Heating Programme in Scotland (described on pages 144–146).

foundations

Bleaklow House
Howard Town Mill
Glossop SK13 8HT
Tel: 01457 891909
Website: www.foundations.uk.com
The national co-ordinating body for Home Improvement Agencies.

Inland Revenue National Insurance Contributions Office (NICO)

Longbenton
Benton Park Road
Newcastle upon Tyne NE98 1ZZ
Tel: 0191 213 5000
Website: www.inlandrevenue.gov.uk
For information about NI contributions and records. The Inland Revenue is also responsible for tax credits. To find details of offices

and Inland Revenue Tax Enquiry Centres, look in the phone book under 'Inland Revenue'.

Pensions Advisory Service (OPAS)

11 Belgrave Road
London SW1V 1RB
Helpline: 0845 601 2923
Website: www.opas.org.uk
Offers help and advice about occupational and personal pensions. Will deal directly with the scheme provider if the problem requires. Can also deal with general enquiries about State Pensions.

Royal National Institute of the Blind (RNIB)

105 Judd Street
London WC1H 9NE
Tel: 020 7388 1266
Helpline: 0845 766 9999, weekdays 9.00am–5.00pm
Website: www.rnib.org.uk
The Benefits Advice and Information Team offers advice and information on social security issues for blind and partially sighted people. The phone number in Wales is 029 2045 0440.

Royal National Institute for Deaf People (RNID)

RNID Information Line
19–23 Featherstone Street
London EC1Y 8SL
Tel: 020 7296 8000 (general)
Helpline: 0808 808 0123, 9.00am–5.00pm
Textphone: 0808 808 9000
Website: www.rnid.org.uk
Provides information for deaf people. The phone number in Wales is 029 2033 3034.

For information about national organisations in Scotland, Wales and Northern Ireland, contact the appropriate national Age Concern (addresses on page 183).

Veterans Agency

Norcross
Blackpool FY5 3WP
Tel: 0800 169 2277 (a free call), 8.15am–5.15pm Mondays to Thursdays, 8.15am–4.30pm Fridays.
Website: www.veteransagency.mod.uk
The Veterans Agency is responsible for the War Pensions Scheme and is also the point of contact within the Ministry of Defence for information and advice on issues of concern to veterans and their families.

FURTHER READING

Government leaflets

As well as the leaflets mentioned in *Your Rights*, there is a catalogue of all the social security leaflets produced (Cat1). Social security leaflets should be available from your local social security office, and they are sometimes in libraries, post offices or CABs. Many are also available on the Internet at www.dwp.gov.uk (or www.thepensionservice.gov.uk) The Inland Revenue deals with issues relating to NI contributions. Leaflets on contributions can be obtained from either social security or Inland Revenue offices or on the Internet at www.inlandrevenue.gov.uk Leaflets on help with health costs are available from the Department of Health, PO Box 777, London SE1 6XH, on the Internet at www.doh.gov.uk or by ringing the Health Literature Line on 0800 555 777.

Other publications

For detailed information on services and benefits for disabled people, you may wish to get the *Disability Rights Handbook* 2004–2005, £14.90 (£10 for individuals receiving any State benefits), available from the Disability Alliance, Universal House, 88–94 Wentworth Street, London E1 7SA. Tel: 020 7247 8776. Website: www.disabilityalliance.org

The Disability Alliance also publishes *Claiming Attendance Allowance: A Self-help Guide for Disabled People aged 65 and over*, price £5 (£3 for individuals receiving benefits).

For detailed information on all social security benefits, with reference to the relevant government legislation, you may wish to refer to the 2004–2005 *Welfare Benefits and Tax Credits Handbook*, £32 plus £3.30 post and packing (£7.50 plus £1.30 post and packing for benefit claimants), which is available from the Child Poverty Action Group (CPAG), 94 White Lion Street, London N1 9PF. Tel: 020 7837 7979. Website: www.cpag.org.uk This two-volume book covers both means-tested and non-means-tested benefits.

These books may also be available for reference at your local library.

KEEPING UP TO DATE

This edition of *Your Rights* is based on the information available in March 2004. The benefit levels will normally apply until the first week in April 2005. A new edition of the book will be published next year to cover the period from April 2005 to April 2006. However, sometimes changes are made during the course of a year.

If you would like us to inform you of any major changes introduced before April 2005, please cut off this page and return it to the address below.

Write in with your details if you do not want to cut up the book.

Dear Age Concern

Please send me details about any major changes introduced before April 2005

Name (block letters) _____

Signature _____

Address _____

_____

_____

Postcode _____

Please return to:

Age Concern (May-2 2004)

FREEPOST (SWB 30375)

Ashburton

Devon TQ13 7ZZ

ABOUT AGE CONCERN

This book is one of a wide range of publications produced by Age Concern England, the National Council on Ageing. Age Concern works on behalf of all older people and believes that later life should be fulfilling and enjoyable. For too many this is impossible. As the leading charitable movement in the UK concerned with ageing and older people, Age Concern finds effective ways to change that situation.

Where possible, we enable older people to solve problems themselves, providing as much or as little support as they need. A network of local Age Concerns, supported by many thousands of volunteers, provides community-based services such as lunch clubs, day centres and home visiting.

Nationally, we take a lead role in campaigning, parliamentary work, policy analysis, research, specialist information and advice provision, and publishing. Innovative programmes promote healthier lifestyles and provide older people with opportunities to give the experience of a lifetime back to their communities.

Age Concern is dependent on donations, covenants and legacies.

Age Concern England
1268 London Road
London SW16 4ER
Tel: 020 8765 7200
Fax: 020 8765 7211
Website:
www.ageconcern.org.uk

Age Concern Cymru
4th Floor
1 Cathedral Road
Cardiff CF11 9SD
Tel: 029 2037 1566
Fax: 029 2039 9562
Website:
www.accymru.org.uk

Age Concern Scotland
113 Rose Street
Edinburgh EH2 3DT
Tel: 0131 220 3345
Fax: 0131 220 2779
Website:
www.ageconcernscotland.org.uk

Age Concern Northern Ireland
3 Lower Crescent
Belfast BT7 1NR
Tel: 028 9024 5729
Advice line: 028 9032 5055
(9.30am–1pm)
Fax: 028 9023 5497
Website: www.ageconcernni.org

PUBLICATIONS FROM AGE CONCERN BOOKS

Money matters

Your Taxes and Savings 2004–2005: A Guide for Older People
Paul Lewis

This definitive annual guide to financial planning for older people:

- is fully revised and updated
- explains the tax system in clear, concise language
- describes the range of saving and investment options available
- includes model portfolios to illustrate a range of financial scenarios

Your Taxes and Savings explains how the tax system affects older people, including how to avoid paying more tax than necessary.
£5.99 0-86242-395-3

Using Your Home as Capital 2004–2005: A Guide to Raising Money from the Value of Your Home
Cecil Hinton and Mark Goodale

This best-selling book for homeowners, which is updated annually, gives a detailed explanation of how to capitalise on the value of your home and obtain additional income.
£4.99 0-86242-396-1

Your Guide to Pensions 2005: Planning Ahead to Boost Retirement Income
Sue Ward

Many older people in their later working lives become concerned about the adequacy of their existing pension arrangements. This annually updated title addresses these worries and suggests strategies to enhance the value of a prospective pension.
£6.99 0-86242-397-X

184

General

Managing Debt: A Guide for Older People

Edited by Yvonne Gallacher and Jim Gray

A significant proportion of older people continue to experience financial problems in retirement. This comprehensive book aims to help those people break free from the vicious debt cycle. It provides information, advice and guidance on managing debt. Topics covered in detail include:

- getting into debt
- negotiating with creditors
- money advice
- prioritising debts and dealing with emergencies
- bankruptcy
- understanding the law and your rights

Written in clear, jargon free language, the book contains examples, sample letters, case studies and a glossary of terms, and is a complete self-help guide for people with financial problems.

£7.99 0-86242-236-1

Changing Direction: Employment Options in Mid-life: 2nd edition

Sue Ward

Redundancy or early retirement can come as a shock to anybody, but the impact in mid-life can be devastating. The new edition of this topical and highly practical book is designed to help those aged 40–55 get back to work. Always positive and upbeat, it examines issues such as adjusting to change, finances, opportunities for work, deciding what work you really want to do and working for yourself.

£9.99 0-86242-331-7

Your Guide to Retirement

Ro Lyon

A comprehensive handbook for older people on the point of retirement, this book is full of practical information and advice on all the opportunities available. It also points readers in the right direction to obtain more information when required. Drawing on Age Concern's wealth of experience, it covers everything you need to know, including:

- managing your money
- staying healthy
- making the most of your time
- housing options
- relationships

Your Guide to Retirement is easy to use and designed to encourage everyone to view retirement as an opportunity not to be missed.

£7.99 0-86242-350-3

The Carers Handbook Series

The Carers Handbook series has been written for the families and friends of older people. It guides readers through key care situations and aims to help them make informed, practical decisions. All the books in the series:

- offer step-by-step guidance on decisions which need to be taken
- examine all the options available
- include practical checklists and case studies
- point you towards specialist help
- are up to date with recent guidelines and issues
- draw on Age Concern's wealth of experience

The Carer's Handbook: What to do and who to turn to
Marina Lewycka   £6.99   0-86242-366-X

Choices for the carer of an elderly relative
Marina Lewycka   £6.99   0-86242-375-9

Caring for someone with a sight problem
Marina Lewycka   £6.99   0-86242-381-3

Caring for someone with cancer
Toni Battison   £6.99   0-86242-382-1

Caring for someone with arthritis
Jim Pollard   £6.99   0-86242-373-2

Caring for someone with diabetes
Marina Lewycka   £6.99   0-86242-374-0

Caring for someone with a heart problem
Toni Battison   £6.99   0-86242-371-6

Caring for someone at a distance
Julie Spencer-Cingöz   £6.99   0-86242-367-8

Caring for someone with an alcohol problem
Mike Ward   £6.99   0-86242-372-4

Caring for someone who is dying
Penny Mares   £6.99   0-86242-370-8

Caring for someone with dementia
Jane Brotchie   £6.99   0-86242-368-6

Caring for someone who has had a stroke
Philip Coyne & Penny Mares   £6.99   0-86242-369-4

Caring for someone with a hearing loss
Marina Lewycka   £6.99   0-86242-380-5

Caring for someone with depression

Toni Battison   £6.99   0-86242-347-4

Caring for someone with memory loss

Toni Battison   £6.99   0-86242-358-9

If you would like to order any of these titles, please write to the address below, enclosing a cheque or money order for the appropriate amount (plus £1.99 p&p for one book; for additional books please add 75p per book up to a maximum of £7.50) made payable to Age Concern England. Credit card orders may be made on 0870 44 22 120. Books can also be ordered online at www.ageconcern.org.uk/shop

Age Concern Books

Units 5 and 6
Industrial Estate
Brecon
Powys LD3 8LA

Bulk order discounts

Age Concern Books is pleased to offer a discount on orders totalling 50 or more copies of the same title. For details, please contact Age Concern Books on 0870 44 22 120.

Customised editions

Age Concern Books is pleased to offer a free 'customisation' service for anyone wishing to purchase 500 or more copies of the title. This gives you the option to have a unique front cover design featuring your organisation's logo and corporate colours, or adding your logo to the current cover design. You can also insert an additional four pages of text for a small additional fee. Existing clients include many of the biggest names in British industry, retailing and finance, the trades unions, educational establishments, the statutory and voluntary sectors, and welfare associations. For full details, please contact Sue Henning, Age Concern Books, Astral House, 1268 London Road, London SW16 4ER. Fax: 020 8765 7211. Email: hennins@ace.org.uk

Visit our website at www.ageconcern.org.uk/shop

INDEX

BENEFIT RATES APRIL 2004–2005

Some of the main weekly benefit rates are listed below for quick reference:

Attendance Allowance

higher rate	£58.80
lower rate	£39.35

Carer's Allowance £44.35

Disability Living Allowance

care component	highest rate	£58.80
	middle rate	£39.35
	lowest rate	£15.55
mobility component	higher rate	£41.05
	lower rate	£15.55

Housing Benefit/Council Tax Benefit standard applicable amounts for people aged 65 and over

single person	£121.00
couple	£181.20

Incapacity Benefit (long-term rate) £74.15

Pension Credit standard appropriate amounts and Housing Benefit/Council Tax Benefit applicable amounts for people aged 60–64*

single person	£105.45
couple	£160.95

Pension Credit maximum savings credit

single person	£15.51
couple	£20.22

Severe Disablement Allowance (basic rate) £44.80

State Pension

basic rate £79.60

wife on husband's contributions £47.65

couple on husband's contributions £127.25

*See pages 47–55 for details of other premiums/additions and housing costs which may give rise to higher rates.

We hope that this publication has been useful to you. If so, we would very much like to hear from you. Alternatively, if you feel that we could add or change anything, then please write and tell us, using the following Freepost Address: Age Concern, FREEPOST CN1 794, LONDON SW16 4BR.